# UNIVERSITY
# OF
# WINNIPEG

**Presented by**

United College Class of '27.

✻

Jones Very: Selected Poems

Jones Very: Selected Poems

Jones Very at 25, from a daguerreo-
type

Jones Very in 1870
*Courtesy of Essex Institute, Salem, Mass.*

❈

# Jones Very: Selected Poems

❈

*Edited and with an Introduction*

*by*

NATHAN LYONS

Rutgers University Press
*New Brunswick    New Jersey*

For Austin Warren

# Acknowledgments

I am grateful to the following libraries, publishers, and historical societies for permission to use and to quote from published and unpublished material in their possession on Jones Very:

Houghton Mifflin Company: poems from *Poems and Essays* (1886), *Poems by Jones Very* (1883); selections from *Journals of Ralph Waldo Emerson*. Duke University Press: poems first published in William Irving Bartlett's *Jones Very: Emerson's Brave Saint*. The Essex Institute, Salem, Massachusetts: manuscript sermon dated ?1860. Wellesley Library: selections from "Epistles to the Unborn" and manuscript letter to Emerson dated 30 November 1838. Harvard College Library, Harvard University: manuscript poems and selections from a letter to Frederick Goddard Tuckerman, dated "Salem, 1861"; also selections from manuscript sermons. Archives, Widener Library, Harvard University: passages from "commonplace" books. Massachusetts Historical Society, Boston, Massachusetts: sections from manuscript letter to H. W. Bellows dated 29 December 1838, and sections from manuscript account by Samuel Gray Ward of a visit from Very. Harris Collection of American Poetry, John

Hay Library, Brown University: manuscript poems and selections from manuscript sermons.

The facsimile of Jones Very's signature on the front cover appears with the permission of the Harvard College Library.

I should like to thank Donald Hall, James R. Squires, and Anthony E. Herbold, for suggestions and criticisms. Particularly, I am deeply grateful to Professor Austin Warren, who introduced me to the poetry of Jones Very and who directed me in this study in ways for which I shall be thankful always.

# CONTENTS

✹

# Jones Very: Selected Poems

# Brief Chronology

1813. August 28, born in Salem, Massachusetts.

1824. Death of Captain Jones Very, the poet's father.

1826. Town award for "exemplary conduct, proficiency, and diligence" at the public school.

1827. Begins work in Salem auction house as errand and store boy.

?1832. Assistant, until entering Harvard, at the Latin School, presided over by Henry K. Oliver.

1834. Enters Harvard in February as a second-semester sophomore.

1836. A.B. degree. Very delivers his essay, "Individuality," as the English Oration at graduation.

1837. Tutor in Greek and theological student at the Harvard Divinity School.

1838. Meets Emerson at Concord in April.
July 15, Emerson's address at the Harvard Divinity School.
In September, withdraws from Harvard during period of heightened religious enthusiasm.
From September 17 to October 17, at McLean Asylum in Somerville.

1839. *Essays and Poems*, published by Little and Brown; selected by Emerson.

1843. Licensed to preach by the Cambridge Association of Ministers, though he first preached in 1842.
Until his death, Very lived in the family house—154 Federal Street—in Salem. He preached more than 100 sermons—one to twenty-one times each—usually on Boston's North Shore, but as far off as Providence, R.I., and Maine.

1880. May 8, death, in Salem.

# *INTRODUCTION*

It is not easy to find a man who has
worked for three years without aiming at pay.
—Confucius

## I

## THE MAN

### (1813–1880)

The poems of Jones Very, the saintly Unitarian clergyman,
report a unique religious experience. A Quietist, Very claimed
that the hand and foot that stir not would find, in their absolute obedience to the will of God, their rightful place to go. A
descendant of Puritans, he was zealous, plain, and militantly
austere; he was intensely loyal to the Bible. Though he valued community, Very advised and quarreled with the disobedient; he sometimes denied Christian brotherhood, fiercely
pronouncing, "I have no brother." Yet he had a peculiar
sweetness, and as a mystic who had known the "new birth,"
he sang the joys of his bright clear morning. Very's unjustly

neglected poems are unparalleled in their grave, spare, un-compromising voice.

The voice is insistent, authoritative. It pleads not by argument, but by its firm and somber tone. Believing that his poems were dictated by the Holy Spirit, that he was God-directed in all things, great and small,[1] Very could say, "I value these verses, not because they are *mine*, but because they are *not*."[2] Very was a specialist within a limited class of emotions: his authority is commitment to a passive search for God that was stringently lived.

Very's life—that of an ascetic or saint—sharply contrasts to the seafaring tradition of his Yankee forefathers. The poet's parents, Captain Jones Very and Lydia Very, were cousins, descendants of a Bridget Very who had settled near Danvers, Massachusetts, before 1643; his ancestors fought the Narragansett Indians, were Revolutionary soldiers, and had taken to sea as a family profession by 1736.[3]

Few unusual events mark Very's exterior life. The tall, slender, and solitary poet studied at Harvard and acted briefly as Tutor in Greek while enrolled at the Divinity School. He was licensed to preach in 1843; then, for nearly forty years he lived modestly at home in his native Salem, preaching his hundred-odd sermons at Unitarian churches in Maine, Rhode Island, and Massachusetts.[4] His one known interior crisis occurred in 1838, when he was "commanded" to banish willful actions, and experienced what he termed the "new birth"; extreme exaltation at this time, while a Tutor, impelled a month's rest at the McLean Asylum in Somerville.

Unlike Emerson, Very was not a diarist. Instead of journals in which one charts his own psychograph, Very compiled "commonplace" books.[5] In these he set down rules, facts, quotations, and opinions with which he rarely quarreled. His first books, begun about 1834, display extraordinary scholastic ambition, and mark an early devotion to *belles-lettres*.[6] There is a four-page entry headed, "On the Formation of a Stile." He knew Samuel P. Newman's *Rhetoric* well, and copied out George Campbell's rules of style from *Philosophy of Rhetoric*. He particularly notes, what he probably learned from Edward Tyrrell Channing at Harvard, the need to "compose frequently and with care." He translated Cicero into French and from French back into Latin, comparing the final effort with the original.

At Harvard, Milton became Very's image of the severe student, and the central figure in his first Bowdoin Prize essay, "The Practical Application in This Life, by Men as Social and Intellectual Beings, of the Certainty of a Future State."[7] Very was not an untutored clairvoyant: his reading was extensive. His "commonplace" books reveal his alert and varied concern with philosophy, theology, and literature, but sometimes an uncritical generosity for inferior talents. He read and seems to have admired Byron, Burns, Prior, Coleridge, Cowper, Joseph Buckminster's "literary" sermons, Sir James Mackintosh's *Dissertation on the Progress of Ethical Philosophy* (and a life of Mackintosh), Isaac Taylor's popular *Natural History of Enthusiasm*, William Henry Furness's *Remarks on the Four Gospels* (read by most Transcendentalists), Robert Pollok's long, dull poem, *The Course of Time*, and Mrs. Hemans' sweet *Memoires*. He praised James Thomson's *The Seasons* as "glorious enthusiasm," and called Bryant "our own great poet." He particularly loved Wordsworth, to whom his early poems are surely indebted, and whom he quotes often both in the "commonplace" books

and later in the sermons. But Very quarrels with Wordsworth's assertion that the poet writes under the "necessity of
giving immediate pleasure to a human being." Replying,
Very echoes a previously quoted passage from William Ellery Channing's "National Literature": "Literature depends
on individual genius, and this, though fostered, cannot be
created by outward helps"; [8] Very insists that there is no such
necessity to give pleasure, but that "his soul has been framed
that it cannot act upon anything without stamping it with its
own press."

A curious logic links the early endorsement of discrete "individual genius" with Very's eventual reliance upon a Divine
Author. For William Ellery Channing, the former term had
been equated with that which is natural or innate. But for
Very the Self became God in us. "To become natural," he
says in his key essay, "Shakespeare," "to find again that Para-
dise which he has lost, man must be born again, he must learn
the true exercise of his own will is only in listening to that
voice which is ever walking in the garden, but of which he is
afraid and hides himself." [9] The merely physical birth must
be supplanted by the "second" or "new" birth. To be natural
is not merely to be animal or merely innocent, but to be
obedient and submissive. Therefore, to be natural, either con-
sciously or unconsciously, is to be great, "for that which is so
is God's." [10] In "Epic Poetry," Very claimed that "the heroism
of Christianity is not seen so much in the outward act, as in
the struggle of the will to control the springs of action." [11]
Obedience is will-lessness, and renunciation of the will allows
God, as the Quakers would have it, to work through and in
the man. Even Shakespeare is justified, because he is "not so
much a man as a natural phenomenon"; his mind, "phenom-

6

enal and unconscious" was, for Very, "almost as much a passive instrument as the material world." Unlike his "unconscious" Shakespeare, however, Very's dictation from the Holy Spirit was tempered by a personal and inflexible ethic. Very called himself a "Channing Unitarian," but he supplants Channing's broad, rational humanism with an illiberal and exacting system that alone can lead to union with God; its central tenet, submission to God's will, has been isolated from Channing's theology as well as from traditional Christianity, and has been given exaggerated importance. This becomes his "great fact," resulting, by his own account, in the great interior "change of heart" that led to brief confinement in an asylum in 1838.

A rare attempt at self-analysis, several months after Very's confinement, reveals as much in its manner as it does in the statements which describe his change and explain his crisis. The letter, to the Reverend H. W. Bellows, his former colleague at the Divinity School, is a valuable document, worth quoting at length.[12] "You probably heard rumors," he writes, "in relation to my leaving Cambridge the truth of which I am now to testify. From what you knew of me before you are aware that my effort was ever to purify my soul and that I was soiled by suffering to make this my constant work. In my senior year in college I experienced what is commonly called a *change of heart*, which tells us that all we have belongs to God and that we ought to have no *will* of our own."

So severe was this belief that, says he, "as long as I had a thought of what I ought to banish I felt that some of my will remained." And he adds, "during the two years succeeding my senior . . . I maintained this conflict—it began with the day and was continued into the night—the enemy gradually

7

yielded and I went on rejoicing to the close." He thought that he had "nothing more to give up to," but in the third week of the new term at Cambridge, he felt a "new will." "It seemed like my old will," he says, "only it was to do good—it was not a feeling of my own but a sensible will that was not my own." Through it he felt a kinship to all with whom he spoke, since, as he says, they were created by "that which" created him.

Then he was led to declare to all that "the coming of Christ was at hand," [13] and he says that this caused him to be placed, contrary to his will, in the asylum. He compares his "new birth" to hearing St. John the Baptist in the wilderness, purification through obedience, and the decrease of John, or the flesh, and the increase of Christ.[14] "I have been in the heart of the earth," he says, "obedient to John three days and three nights and am risen in Christ as a witness unto you and all that he comes not by water only but by blood."

At Harvard, Very had been shy and rigorous, his voice increasingly anagogical as this sense of mission emerged. The practical and sober eye of Samuel Gray Ward, who later managed the financing of the Alaska Purchase, saw Very as "intensely self-conscious," "solemn," with a "not-to-be-trifled-with-awkwardness"; Ward saw in his face a "peculiarly sweet and compassionate expression," and a constant nervous twitching that checked his words.[15] Most interesting is the highly evangelic tone recalled by Ward. The banker and the poet-mystic sat side by side in classes for three years with but little discourse. In 1839 Very suddenly visited Ward, to "lay the axe" at his door. He invited Ward to "the feast, where all are gathered." He said that the wheat must be separated from the husk. Then, noting that Ward was writing a letter, he said: "If you are ready, break it off and follow me." But the banker, no doubt wary of messianic pronouncements, assured him that he was not ready, that he had a letter to write, and a life to live, that he considered husks both "beautiful and useful." Very said he would soon have a "new mansion" for himself. The practical Ward asked if he spoke of his temporal or spiritual house. Very replied that it was all one, there was "but one house."

That Very was rapt and committed, there can be no doubt. He lived his Bible; like the Puritan or Quaker, he accepted its phraseology and brought it to each moment of his life. He began to live with the sure sense that he had achieved holiness. The Reverend James Freeman Clarke, who later solicited and published Very's poems in the *Western Messenger*, records what may have been the first meeting of Channing and Very. Channing had noted that while Very spoke he had left his chair and rested his arm on the mantel. He asked: "Did you do this of your own accord or in obedience to the Spirit?" Very answered, "In obedience to the Spirit."[16] And since these actions and his words were not his own, Very could insist that they were not personal but the Truth, that they were "no more disputable than . . . the blowing of this south wind."[17]

One can scarcely doubt the subjective reality of the experience for Very. It led him to "unhorse" a local preacher, to direct incisive remarks at the "respectable pillars of the churches in Salem," and to seek out local clergymen that they might pray with him and be saved.[18] Thus the biting antagonism within Very between the communal aspect of established religion and his own rigorous tenets sometimes pro-

9

duced desolation and even misanthropy. Very wanted to love, but could not love those who "borrow words for thoughts they cannot feel,/That with a seeming heart their tongue may speak" ("The Dead"). Christianity enjoins community, but friends and family must be left when Christ calls. In "The Narrow Way," Very finds "no friend and yet a friend in all to greet." Though he addresses many poems to "my brother," his brutal vision in "The Eagles," the slaughter there of the unregenerate, suggests that his own sense of brotherhood lay chiefly with those who did not "Offer a hand with their own wills defiled" ("Thy Brother's Blood"). Though Very was ten years Emerson's junior, his achieved Truth led him to try to become Emerson's spiritual director. Very told him bluntly that he "saw the truth better than others," but that his spirit was "not quite right"; and he directly proselytized Emerson, sending him a number of formal "Epistles to the Unborn." Assurance of his own holiness gave Very a sweetness and an authority; but the latter often makes us as uncomfortable as the local "pillars." At once distasteful or amusing or just, implying high spiritual pride or merely conviction, they demonstrate the ageless problem of the seer. Deeply resentful of observed hypocrisy or spiritual impotence, is he entitled to reject and badger all who have not met his own rigid, perhaps even arbitrary, vision? Does he have, as Monsignor Knox asks of Quietists in general, a "monopoly of the love of God"? [19] Or a monopoly on an elusive truth? Clearly, Very thought he did.

This belief, the strict way in which it was lived, and his strange personal relationship with Emerson has made contrast inevitable, a contrast which helps to distinguish Very from the Transcendentalists, with whom he is wrongly catalogued. [20]

The pivotal difference between Very and Emerson is not that one was a relativist, the other an absolutist; it is their temperaments, and their valuing of God and man. Emerson was not a relativist, but a syncretist. All things, he said in *Nature*, are ancillary to a man. For Very, all things were ancillary to God; like Jonathan Edwards, he posited a God glorified in man's dependence. Both Very and Emerson would surrender themselves, but for Very this meant abandoning the self, and for Emerson it meant gaining it. Emerson sought to exploit man's infinite potential by allowing him to participate in the unconscious world beyond him; he would also have a man know his own worth, and keep things under his feet; rather than skulk or peep about like a bastard or an interloper in a world that existed for him, man should gain, through self-reliance, a world and a self. Emerson sought to make man, through abandonment, the notorious "transparent eyeball" that took in the rich variegation of the outside world. Since the natural world is filled with paradox, so would be the full man. Emerson thus endorsed Nature as a principal source of wisdom, and envisioned in it an impersonal God. Very not only knew a personal God to be immanent, but in his ecstasy identified himself with the Savior and the Holy Spirit.[21] He sharply quarreled with those who called Nature the "Older Scriptures," and said that "the testimony of the natural world is external to ourselves and cannot fully enlighten the mind."[22] Emerson was more alert to the texture of a man's mind, its layers of content, than to its single truth or falsity; rather, perhaps, he sought to equate truth and texture. Very allowed a personal and single Voice to speak through him. He also sought wholeness for man; he wanted him to live not in one room, or in one hole "like skulking mouse," but fully in the "house" of Christianity, and thus walk humbly again with his God.[23]

Emerson prized various processes of thought, and valued that which was independently achieved; he quarreled with, in his secular realm, what Very also eschewed: second-hand communion with a thought or a Deity. But Very strictly opposed the idea that "truth is what each mind conceives it." If man is the Truth, then, Emerson might have argued, what enters him and adds to it only makes this Truth larger; even perception of God's Truth is tempered by a meddlesome subjectivity. For Very, man had to love and be obedient if he would experience the one Truth; for Emerson, man had at once to expand and preserve the sacred integrity of his own soul. One held fast to a philosophy of "being," the other "becoming."[24] Very had to detach himself from others and from things to remain honest to his genius; Emerson required and championed generous conversation.[25]

To raise man, Emerson chose an open-ended philosophic idealism; to glorify God, Very lived a narrow version of the revealed Gospel. Very had one fact, Emerson a thousand. For Emerson, Christ could only be a great prophet, only in a metaphorical sense an incarnation of God;[26] for Very, there could be no Christianity without a belief in the resurrection.[27] Unitarianism, rejecting Calvinist predetermination and Catholic mysteries, had found an approach to salvation in individual reason. Emerson rebelled, ranging afield, seeking a new, more commodious, a warmer spirit. Very went directly to the Godhead; the Gospel, and finally local pulpits sufficed.

But the visions of Emerson and Very, each divorced from materialism, form a rich spiritual dichotomy. If man negates his self he may negate his talents and have nothing to present

12

when his Master returns; if he negates God he may negate the vision of all which transcends him. Though neither way of life could finally accept the other, the two need not be antagonistic: glorification of God may best proceed by non-attachment, but it need not humiliate man. If the best in man is "God's seed," and if man is God's handiwork, then evidence of this seed is evidence of God, and to glorify man might also be to glorify God. Very's achievement is his verse and his life; he chose, like Thomas à Kempis, a life of detachment, utter humility, purity. Ultimately, already isolated from most of his contemporaries by the severity of his vision, Very disappointed Emerson; his narrow way had to be supplanted by a road as broad and generous as that of Walt Whitman.

But Emerson, with his eye for esthetic values, had recognized Very's literary talent. In 1839, genuinely fond of his "brave saint's" poems, he selected and edited a small volume of verse from Very's most prolific period. Reputedly, Very composed in a bare, austere room under the gambrel roof of his home, "The Prophet's Chamber," and in the sloping garden behind the house, at a spot his family called "Inspiration Point." [28] Monotonously he would tap against the lattice work as he composed, often making one or two poems a day. Many were written in a small rapid scrawl on large sheets of paper, neatly folded twice.[29] A sheet could contain as many as thirty-two poems. Many lack punctuation and have other resemblances to automatic (or impatient) writing. The earliest poems show the influence of late eighteenth-century verse, probably Cowper's; his blank verse mingles Wordsworthian heightened-prose with Miltonic overstatement and inversion.[30] There are a few hymns, short poems in couplet or inter-

13

locking couplet; then, for several years, mostly sonnets. A moderate number of the sonnets, chiefly the religious poems, have their own voice, a voice rarely similar to that of any other poet. These are his best work and nearly all are from his "great period," his years of religious excitation—at most, from 1836 to 1841.

Writing in 1861 to his former pupil, the poet Frederick Goddard Tuckerman, Very says: "I am not engaged in any literary work. I write occasionally for the Salem Gazette, The Christian Register, and The Monthly Religious Magazine. I have since 1842 been a preacher of the Gospel." [31] A preacher of the Gospel—how complete and apt a description of his change. How far Very had separated himself from the great names: his former professors, George Ticknor, Edward Everett, and E. T. Channing—and from Emerson. He was now, vocationally and professionally, a divine. In the early 1840's Very's reading became more markedly theological. It included Quaker thought, sermons, and devotional literature. He read George Fox, John Woolman, *The Life of William Penn* by Thomas Clarkson, and Penn's letters. His last "commonplace" book includes long selections from Henry Millman's *History of Christianity* and St. Basil's "Homily on Faith." About this time Very became more cautious towards literature: he sought the humble and pious tenor, rather than the brilliant. He copied out selections from George Herbert's "The Parson on Sundays," and "The Parson in Sacraments"; he copied all of Henry Vaughan's "Early Rising and Prayer." He sought not only moral justification for poetry, as he did in "Shakespeare" and "Hamlet," but a practical way to live humbly and devoutly in the world. His final and perhaps most important entry, probably written in 1843 or 1844, is a long series of quotations from *The Principles of the Interior or Hidden Life* (1843) by Thomas C. Upham. Upham was greatly influenced by the French Quietists, Fénelon and Mme. Guyon, and phrases like, "he is at rest, but never idle," match Very's own earlier tenets.[32] But though Very may have found support in Quakerism and in Upham's prescriptions for the interior life, though he perhaps found an image in Herbert and the sermons he read for the life he now entered, his religion was already formed.

Jones Very first preached in 1842. Though his hesitating voice and low monotone never made him a popular preacher, or perhaps even an effective one, Very's sermons were the major effort of his last thirty-odd years. He often directly paralleled themes in verse and sermon: the logos, justification by faith, the unity of all sects. The sermon statement, now more germane, invariably surpasses the poem.

Very's genius lay not in sustained discourse but in assigning form to his religious experience. His sermons are thus less extraordinary than his earlier, short poems. In the sermons he is less intensely loyal to that first vision; he does not compromise it, but is less apocalyptic, quicker to explain and to distinguish. He asserts in one sermon that arguments on Trinitarianism substitute reasoning for faith and imitation of Christ, that they demonstrate "vain curiosity and intellectual pride"; [33] but he goes on to insist upon and demonstrate the Unity of God. He argues the unity of all sects, but quarrels with Catholic unity built on "fear, oppression, and ignorance."

Some sermons attest to broader sympathies. He praises civilization, science, and "well-directed mental and physical behavior." He links religious goals both to the individual and

15

the nation. He quotes Milton, Edmund Waller, Coleridge, Wordsworth, and Burns, and uses anecdotes about Alexander, Xerxes, and Greenlanders, after the manner of many another nineteenth-century literary preacher. He even lapses into un-rhymed poetry.

Other sermons show his capacity for capable theological distinctions: between the hesitancy of Thomas and that of Paul; [34] between the illusion of spiritual participation in the unseen, and the rigorous preparation necessary for that partici-pation; [35] between the potential burden the Church places on personal faith and love, and the necessity of the Church in the "Divine Economy"; [36] between foolish expectation and humble dependence, credulousness and trust; [37] between the ascetic's pride in his austerities, and belief in the primacy of the soul; [38] between the natural eyes of Mark, Matthew, and Luke, and John's inward discernment of Christ; [39] between intellectualized religion, and living the life of the Savior; [40] and, aptly, between injurious fanaticism, and needed enthu-siasm.[41]

In short, Very broadened, admitted paradox, became more genial, and mingled with the things and issues of the world. But when he became more human, more interested in prag-matic problems and more capable of arguing them and syn-thesizing them with his religion, he also became something of another person; and this person, though he may have been more commodious, was not a poet; when Very strayed from his severely narrow vision, his poems became trite and com-monplace. The poems arose, as for Wordsworth, out of the early and the deep; when adjusted, even slightly, by prag-matic reason, his poetic vision, already limited, exhausted itself. Very later spoke to so many people that his voice changed from the haunting and intimidating voice of his poetic vision to that of a pious but rarely exceptional clergyman. His genius for registering in poetry the intensity of his early, special insights produced his most enduring work.

## II

## THE POETRY

The Quietist image will not admit much exploration, in deference to its ethic as well as its scope. Very's stylistic canon is therefore sharply limited. The Shakespearean sonnet is his predominant form; curt Biblical syntax and regular meter encourage slow, measured reading; paradox, simple metaphor, and metonymy are the principal figures; chaste imagery supplies the slightest color and animation to his verse.

Very's poems are without drama; for drama is of the world, and Very is hardly a creaturely poet. Paradox provides the only drama of Christian mysticism: he that will save his life, must first lose it; he that will lose his life for Christ's sake, shall find it; the last shall be the first; when man is weak, then is he strong; in death begins eternal life; to him who hath shall be given. As a poet and an intense Christian mystic, Very has sure recourse to this rich lode. But his poems are rarely mystical; though many were written in what he claims was mystical communion, they generally only state his mystical paradoxes.

Very's paradox is never pointed or sharp. The oxymoron of Crashaw's epigrams or Donne's Holy Sonnets demonstrate an intellectual, even an emotional, vigor opposed to Very's Quietism; poetic success in these terms would have undermined the man. Very resolves traditional quarrels between matter and spirit, motion and rest, life and death, not by violently yoking them, but by quiet and authoritative reconciliation. He uses antithetical parallels within one line, or in one line against the next—closer, in this, to neoclassic than metaphysical prosody. At their worst, Very's paradoxes are merely undistinguished echoes of Biblical passages: "For those who worship Thee there is no death." At their best, they convince, leisurely establishing the central paradox of passive-seeking:

> These when they come, the man revealed from heaven,
> Shall labor all the day in quiet rest.
>
> ("The New Man")

and,

> It is the way unseen, the certain route,
> Where ever bound, yet thou art ever free.
>
> ("The Hand and Foot")

Very's is a hidden God. For communion with Him, the poet cherishes only the intangible. In one sermon, he speaks of "this tyranny of what is seen"; self-denial is prayer; and one can pray only when he prays inwardly. In "Enoch," the poet looks to find a man who walked with God:

> But soul forgetful of her nobler birth
> Had hewn Him lofty shrines of stone and wood,
> And left unfinished and in ruins still
> The only temple He delights to fill.

Like the Wesleyan and the Quaker, Very insists upon first-hand religion: there can be neither physical nor personal intermediaries.

For communion, and to find the "meat" that does not perish, man must be reborn. But first he must be "self-forgetting." From this proceeds Very's special concept of surrender. It has not the sponge-like quality of Whitman's loafing. It is a "wise-passiveness," but it excludes Wordsworth's connotation that what is received from nature is a principal source of ethical knowledge. Very differs with the Indian religions, particularly Buddhism, in that he expects no noetic satori, no sudden perception of an ultimate reality. Very's surrender is the motion of thought within rest, the peace of "traveling" on his "Maker's river": but mainly it is a disinterested act of devotion to the Father.

Such a surrender implies a willful decision to be will-less; in Anthony Herbold's admirable phrase, "a willed will-less-ness." But this scarcely invalidates the premises of Very's Quietism. "The Hand and Foot" is the perfect inscription to Very's religion, and it remains a focal poem for the study of his central paradox. Though the first two lines imply an initial conscious choice, the focus is upon the process once initiated.

> The hand and foot that stir not, they shall find
> Sooner than all, the rightful place to go.

There is a kind of justification by selflessness. Such a view is not Calvinist, for it implies no elected soul; the soul is set free through its peculiar holiness, its total surrender, as any other soul might be set free. Very sought and contributed to his salvation; it was not an imputed righteousness.

"Rightful place" might imply that no other path is possible; but such stress would be wrong. The phrase states, not that no other choice exists, but that this absolute can be reached by a process, at this moment extrinsic to choice. All movement and thought might imply conscious exercise of will, even the movement of a hand or the conjuring of an idea. But in Very's canon, thought is simply received, and acts are directed; this, after the initial, general abandonment. "Thou wilt my hand employ," he begins "The Disciple"; and "I idle stand that I may find employ," he affirms in "The Idler." Though Knox can caution that in the mystical state man has the illusion that he is an automaton, the "other power" directing Very to the "rightful place" was a paramount assumption. Again, only the initial submission could be willed: "The morning comes to those who willingly would see." And selflessness could be willed: "We must by an effort of the will, by prayer, and meditation, turn the mind from vanity and worldliness, before the Truth can interest us, enter into and fill the soul."

Consequently, spiritual vigor is constantly contrasted to restless and selfish physical labor; the decrease in the latter is requisite to the initiation of any spiritual moment. Very's unseen God cannot be found in outward activity; repeatedly, busyness keeps man from communion.

> Nor here nor there, where now thy feet would turn,
> Thou wilt find Him who ever seeks for thee.
>
> ("The Created")

Only stillness evokes the knowledge of direction:

> My body shall not turn which way it will,
> But stand till I the appointed road can find.
>
> ("The Idler")

The only zeal is within the calm:

21

Till to the light restored by gentle sleep
With new-found zeal I might Thy precepts keep.

("Change")

And by seeking Him, one finds himself:

His way is hidden that thine eye may seek,
And in the seeking thou thyself may find.

("To All")

While at rest, man sees by "inward light things hid before";
from the unheard God one learns to speak.

Very's symbols are actually little more than simple meta-
phors, at times metonymies; these become themes, repeated
fugally throughout his work. Often the symbols originate in
a Biblical image or phrase, and retell it, expanding and sus-
taining the original figure. The figure is often in the title
itself. It may combine mild paradox and metonymy: "Christ-
mas" refers more to Easter, to a new birth of Christ, a resurrection in those who were spiritually dead; "The Jew" quarrels with the "thorny talk" of form and convention which
Very equates with Old Testament laws and the rejection of
Christ. "The Journey" is a spiritual pilgrimage; "The Unfaithful Servants" are hands, eyes, and souls that serve themselves, not God; "The Garden" is a state of communion with
God. "The Slaveholder" profiteers with God's free gifts and
holds the day in bonds; "The Children" remain children
of the Father, but have lost all child-like simplicity, humble
love, and thanks. Eye, ear, hand, foot, fox, and bird—among
Very's few physical images—become emblematic of the
poet's quarrel with sense. A most interesting metonymy is
"room," in "The Absent." Because they are separate, and designed for special purposes, rooms are metaphorically com-

pared to men whose lives reflect specialized passions rather than the wholeness of living in the "mansion" of Christianity: "Within thy sleeping room thou dost abide,/And thou the social parlor dost prefer."

The morning, a much used and central image, is spiritual awakening; it comes to those who "willingly would see." "The Clouded Morning" is a time when man should awaken, but does not. In "The Morning Watch," Very follows the physical day from pre-dawn darkness to the flooding of windows with "the awakening light"; but all slumber, there is no faithful herald or watchman to proclaim the dawn, no Christian community—"No friends from house to house their neighbors greet"; all slumber on in sluggard trances; finally, the "day's bright gates" close, and all chance of awakening has passed. The rich sonnet "Morning" first discloses an image of the new day with its noisy workmen, busy laborers in the fields, and an embarking traveler; this Very contrasts to an inner awakening, where too a "light breaks gently." But here,

> The forge and noisy anvil are at rest
> Nor men nor oxen tread the fields of corn,
> Nor pilgrim lifts his staff—it is no day
> To those who find on earth their place to stay.

"The Eagles," a less simply conceived, more rigorously sustained symbolic effort, allegorizes Matthew 24:28: "For wheresoever the carcass is, there will the eagles be gathered together." Eagles are depicted gathering at "the place of death," the air tainted with their "noisome breath." But the poem is not a total metaphorical equivalent for the destruction of the unregenerate; Very slips fluidly into direct statement with justifying abruptness: "But all unburied lies the naked soul," and "The battened wills beneath their talons bleed." He returns to the central image, depicting "whitening bone," "pestilence," and the carcasses; then he becomes suggestively obvious in "half formed prey," and finally the iron beaks pursue their slaughter relentlessly until the field is cleared of those "who worshipped idol gods." The sonnet is graphically mordant; the slaughter fitted to the animality Very eschews; but the evil or sin itself—self-will—is abstract, and never particularized.

Of Very's total poetic achievement—over seven hundred poems—more than 80 per cent are Shakespearean sonnets. Use of a form he did not create probably made the process of writing seem less willful, and may have added to its attractiveness for one who wished to surrender. An early mastery of the form, a respect for order, and the fear of "the weight of too much liberty," are possible reasons for its adoption. Invariably the sonnets are metrically regular (occasionally too facile, even monotonous) and the rhyme correct. Very's basic unit of thought is the line, or more usually, a pair of unrhymed lines. He seems to have built his sonnets by interlocking couplets; first he set down two unrhymed lines, then he found a set to match them.

Very's line is firm and economical; the line is curt, but never, as in Donne, shrewdly so. There is a marked absence of caesuras—in "The Lost," "In Him We Live," and in most other poems. Sometimes Very syncopates an object, "To want is there to be where I am not" ("The Sower"). Often he reverses standard word order. Very likes the Latinic verb-last structure, common to the Protestant hymn; its flexibility helps to explain his ease in the sonnet form, for with it he

24

more easily maintains meter and meets the rhyme. Very pads frequently, often without major damage, in the usual ways, by the use of redundant clauses, and the contrived use of awkward verb forms: "Mid tombs and ruined piles in death to dwell." The end verbs allow him to shift emphasis structurally; at times he juxtaposes related images by use of a subject-object or double object grouping, followed by the verb. Note the rapid succession of object after subject and the suspended verb in, "And long thy life my body shall sustain"; the use of a split verb with a lengthy object inserted, "They cannot from their path mistaken stray"; and the quick repetition of key terms, here a double object in similar construction—"I cannot find in mine own work my joy." The concision of Very's line aptly supports his thrifty religion.

In Very's best poems, the epithets are singularly lean: cunning fox, aged chair, skulking mouse, dim lamp, and thorny talk. His diction is Biblically tight, and often homely. He relies chiefly on one- or two-syllable words. Thee, thou, thine, this, that, here, there, where, He, and Him are used with an accusing directness. Very makes remarkable use of the pronoun, demonstrative and personal, as in the superb poem, "The Created": "Nor here nor there, where now thy feet would turn,/Thou wilt find Him who ever seeks for thee." These strikingly simple lines, which pronounce the threat to spiritual salvation incurred by hurriedness, are equally lean:

While thou wert busy here and there
So He was here and He is gone
Thou oft had time enough to spare
But He thy Lord and Master now.

Very's success in these last lines suggests that tetrameter quatrains might have proved a more flexible form for him than the sonnet. Though a poet who would pad a sonnet might also pad a quatrain, the freer line of Emily Dickinson, or the abrupt distich of the German mystic Angelus Silesius seem more reasonably germane to Very's method; the weight of more liberty might have encouraged closer fidelity to the apocalyptic.

But Very's sonnets, when there is enough matter for the form, are firm and enduring. Among his best are "The Presence," "The Hand and Foot," "The Journey," "In Him We Live," and "The Absent." "The Presence" begins with the ingenuous,

> I sit within my room and joy to find
> That Thou who always lov'st art with me here.

The moment is a state of recognition and quiet thankfulness set in a common scene with some few bare objects. No reason is given for the Divine presence; though there is a watch, there is no sensation of time: there is only unhurried satisfaction in ritual quiet. Very does not prove the presence of God. His authority usually manifests itself in direct statement, neither argued nor debated, often shown. He is master of the abrupt, affirming start: he will bear direct witness to his experience. "I saw the spot where our first parents dwelt," he begins "The Garden"; "I am thy other self"; "I do not need thy food, but thou dost mine"; "I have no brother." Although there is no conscious drama, there is a profound dramatic effect in the unusual juxtaposition of God's indwelling and the perfect stillness of the scene. God's presence (not God) originates in the poet's soul. Channing, who opposed pantheism, says in "Likeness to God": "We see God around us because he dwells within us." [42] For Very, God is external to man; he speaks from without; "but it is *outward from within*," [43] after a man has gently encouraged God's entrance into him. There are parallels to Hinduism and Emerson's "Brahma" in "Thou art the eyes by which I see"; the poet looks with God, and therefore the fire burns brighter. The unadorned things, "The aged chair, that table, watch and door," are part of his large estate, and are sufficient.

The five members of the sonnet are brief and unaffected: the middle three, each neatly of two lines, distinctly note common acts, sights, and things. The nouns are characteristically plain; "aged," the lone adjective, is hardly an extravagance. Very speaks of essentials that do not change, that perform the necessary tasks for man with a quiet holiness, the door that enables him to leave or remain secluded, the table for written thoughts; he ignores fashion; progress for him meant only "new depths of truth within the holy word." [44]

"The Hand and Foot," "The Journey," "In Him We Live," and "The Absent," are more typical sonnets; they do not depict an actual scene, as do "The Fair Morning," and the nature poems: they particularize an idea. The little variety they do contain usually takes the form of alternate images for the central idea.

In "The Hand and Foot," the initial paradox is maintained throughout, restated in different ways, in somber, patient insistence upon the need to submit wholly. Partial parataxis keeps the phrases and members in a delicately elliptical relationship, and encourages the imaginative turning and developing of the first image into distinct images. The slight dis-

27

ruption of word order and the elimination of usual grammatical links in the fifth member enhances the characteristic tightness.

> The bird has not their hidden track found out,
> The cunning fox though full of art he be.

The first image then grows to include the idea that the path is not theirs (is, itself, not willfully chosen); that it is unseen, beyond, as it were, the vision of bird and cunning fox; that it is a bondage that makes them free; and finally, that it is His path, a path thus perfect, for it is made by Him whose perfect law of love "Bids spheres and atoms in just order move."

"The Journey" and "In Him We Live" are more abstract, yet the spare Verian abstract even here reports a convincing belief. Very tells of journeys where he daily walks. Though there is "no end in view," there is an unwillingness to act or plan:

> I know nowhere to turn, each step is new
> No wish before me flies to point the way.

Very never wanted to know the Divine Plan. The conflict here, between man's inevitable ignorance and his need of an absolute path, is resolved, as before, by delivering oneself over to God's will. Though man, "all houseless," knows "not where to dwell," God knows the turnings of the road, "where this way leads and that."

"In Him We Live" has a gently dialectical progression held within the direct affirmation of the first and last two lines. Initially, Very praises the Father, and offers thanks that "in each motion" he is "made rich" with Him. Then there is a development of essentially abstract sense images: a glance, movement of the body, song, movement of the hands. This stately body, Very says, cannot move, "save I/Will to its nobleness my little bring." To sing, he must "consent" to every note; he "must conspire" with every effort to move his hands. But even these little acts of cordial cooperation with the Father are too much: they show him how "little" he possesses, and even that "little," more than he desires.

"The Absent" has a precious intimacy. Its scene, always and obviously metaphoric, is built by domestic and local images. Those who are "not yet at home" have "one hole like rat or skulking mouse," and are blind to all others; they prefer the sleeping room, the parlor, and,

> All others wilt in the cupboard hide,
> And this or that's the room for him or her.

With these homely images, Very connotes the security that accompanies finite man who trusts, and the paltriness of any worldly vision.

Rejection of the incarnated world prevented Very from entering, like his Shakespeare, into the lives of others or of things.[45] There are no characters in his poems, no explicit conflicts, and few scenes. The intangible, alone permanent and holy, reigns supreme. Nature, as for Emerson, is a "differential thermometer," a way of registering man's departure from the natural; and with Swedenborg, Very could say that the visible world was created for our instruction; but the poet's correspondences are too often flat and without form.

Appreciation of natural beauty, as Very implies in "The Lost," "The True Light," and "To the Pure All Things Are Pure," depends upon man's inner awakening, his "sweet obedience of the will." And in "The Lost," Very firmly states that then man can enter into nature:

> Thyself the day thou lookest for in them,
> Thyself the flower that now thine eye enjoys.

But nature was, for Very, more often a source of comfort than revelation and communion, and he rarely entered the portal beyond appearance: nature supplied a ragbag of images from which to draw morals in the manner of the medieval bestiary. The nature poems, although generously praised by some of Very's few admirers, are prosaic and littered with poetic commonplaces and stale epithets; they generally lack the apocalyptic proof of the religious sonnets.[46] In "The Columbine," for example, where Very graphically attempts to show communion with a specific plant, we are not convinced that he and the flower are actually nodding their honey-bells together 'mid pliant grass. And such epithets as "mirrored beauty," "pictured flowers," "boundless main," "morning's golden darting beam," and "stream of life" further mar the nature poems. "The Latter Rain," attempting something less alien to the poet's spirit, is a refreshing exception:

> The rain falls still—the fruit all ripened drops,
> It pierces chestnut burr and walnut shell,
> The furrowed fields disclose the yellow crops,
> Each bursting pod of talents used can tell.

Perhaps because Very did not seek communion, or illumination from Nature's "mystic book," the image has, quite simply, a pristine concreteness.

Some of Very's hymns also have real merit. "The Coming

of the Lord" is among the best, with its strong avowal of abiding faith:

Come suddenly, O Lord, or slowly come,
I wait Thy will, Thy servant ready is;

and its vigorous, taut, conclusion:

Lord, help me that I faint not, weary grow,
Nor at Thy coming slumber too, and sleep;
For Thou hast promised, and full well I know
Thou wilt to us Thy word of promise keep.

"Faith and Sight" richly echoes the morning images:

The comings on of Faith,
    The goings out of Sight;
Are as the brightening of the morn,
    The dying of the night.

And "The Prayer," with its plaintive questioning, and final assurance, and "The Fox and the Bird," which gnomically affirms the primacy of the unseen, are superior performances. "The Coming of the Lord" and "The Immortal" have affinities with the hymns of Isaac Watts, and Cowper's *Olney Hymns*—"Walking With God," for example; the others are more peculiarly Very's.

But it is the religious sonnets which, in theology and style, are unparalleled. Very's theological beliefs were altogether unlike Blake's, with whom he has wrongly been compared. For Blake, finding sex and violence chief ingredients of his world, stated that "God wants not man to humble himself," and persistently argued with brittle and acid pith that life is will. Charles Eliot Norton suggested that Very's poems are "as if written by a George Herbert who had studied Shakespeare, read Wordsworth, and lived in America." [47] Very could be homelier than Herbert, but he lacked Herbert's dazzling variety, his exacting architectonics; more pertinently, Herbert was not a Quietist, and Very was not a metaphysical poet. The Wordsworth of "Expostulation and Reply" and "Michael" is surely a source, but only vaguely a counterpart, particularly not in the religious sonnets or hymns; moreover, Very vitalized conventional devotion, while Wordsworth rejected it; Very was more abstract, more consistently bound to one paradox, and he employed a more static form. Very specially praised William Cullen Bryant's "The Future Life"; his moral nature poems belong, but hardly compare in quality, to the tradition of "To the Fringed Gentian" and "To a Waterfowl." But Bryant's religious poems are more sustained, rhetorical, and aureate. Often Very's flights are so low as to resemble the frequent flat statement of Coventry Patmore, William Collins, and Cowper, but he differs significantly from each. Each voice threatens to, and often does, become dull, trite, and complacently pious. None becomes so laconic as Very, so sure in a few devotional forms, so abjuring of all emotions but one.

Very's failures are obvious and revealing. Though he may seem more a medium than a maker, Very could not have written his sonnets without stringent literary training in his youth. Very's theology falters when it is commonplace or too abstract, but the main flaw is merely faulty poetics. Emerson asked, "Cannot the Spirit parse and spell?" To be faithful to the Spirit which "dictated" his poems—and which has, no doubt a hand in all genuine poetry—Very did not necessarily need to accept its first promptings, but should have argued each poem into a "fidelity to its own nature," however long that might have taken. Knox's observation is apt: "total aban-donment to the Divine will is not inconsistent with having, and with expressing wishes of one's own"; [48] and, it may be added, neither is it inconsistent with artistic awareness. Yeats would have said that Very was too honest. But the act of faith that sometimes cheated Very's art is also the instrument of his great individual achievements.

Very's best poems, culled from a cumbersome and varied assortment, number about seventy and form a unified pattern. I have made, for some convenience, three simple groups: *Obedience*, *For the Disobedient*, and *Song*. The first section establishes the terms of Very's Quietism: passivity, imitation of Christ, submission, and obedience. Here also is the struggle to obey, the confusion and inadequacy to the task, the pain of social rejection, ecstatic "new birth," the voice of the Spirit now in him, the gratitude to the Father, and the joy in His presence. In the second section, the poet seeks others who have achieved holiness; but he is disappointed. He hungers for brotherhood, but admonishes the disobedient. He quarrels here with the substitution of physical for spiritual labor; he suggests the loss of salvation in busyness, but more, a parallel failure to love the source of all being. Very suggests what is required of all, and invites all to be resurrected in Christ; he knows that those who can, will. The final group is short. The poems here are markedly sweeter in tone. Very is thankful for God's gifts. Though his morning is full of joy, and he has some communion with nature, he can still be hesitant or critical; but he employs a gentler voice, a questioning song or hymn. Finally, he praises the unseen, the spiritual, and the Father. [49]

This is Jones Very's world. It is narrow, but it can be calm and deep. There is no physical joy, no sustained ecstasy; Very is deaf to sex and humor. His voice admits no Dickinsonian playfulness; it is at turns patient, thankful, warning, and praising. Sometimes the voice is interior prayer, scarcely audible; but it can acutely chide; always it is sweet, somber, or grave. Unlike Blake's insistence, in poems such as "London," on a broad canon and the specifics of evil, Very's evil is narrow and abstract, limited chiefly to self-will. Very is a dualist, and he does not attempt Thomistically to reconcile the active and the contemplative lives: he explores and extols the motion of contemplation. Very's world is a paean to love of the unseen, and to submission to the Father; we leave it not with a broad theology, but an image of a life solitary and without compromise, intense yet calm, of one carrying his cross without gripe or cheat.

If we live in the incarnated world but neglect it for spiritual aspirations, we are in danger of becoming split, deracinated, transformed, forced into strange skins and deep burrows; if we neglect the spiritual world we court the eagles. Very lives in an upper room, a prophet's or a priest's chamber, and is specially able within a limited class of emotions. But he is antidote and complement to materialism, and frigid witwork, and indecision. Very's world is illiberal, with a monotonic purity. His deep quiet encourages a tight marshalling of inner forces, and within our frantic hurry an intense stillness.

*SELECTED POEMS*
*BY JONES VERY*

# I

## OBEDIENCE

## I

## *The Hand and Foot*

The hand and foot that stir not, they shall find
Sooner than all the rightful place to go:
Now in their motion free as roving wind,
Though first no snail so limited and slow;
I mark them full of labor all the day,
Each active motion made in perfect rest;
They cannot from their path mistaken stray,
Though 'tis not theirs, yet in it they are blest;
The bird has not their hidden track found out,
The cunning fox though full of art he be;
It is the way unseen, the certain route,
Where ever bound, yet thou art ever free;
The path of Him, whose perfect law of love
Bids spheres and atoms in just order move.

## 2

## *The Idler*

I idle stand that I may find employ,
Such as my Master when He comes will give;
I cannot find in mine own work my joy,
But wait, although in waiting I must live;
My body shall not turn which way it will,
But stand till I the appointed road can find,
And journeying so His messages fulfill,
And do at every step the work designed.
Enough for me, still day by day to wait
Till Thou who form'st me find'st me too a task;
A cripple lying at the rich man's gate,
Content for the few crumbs I get to ask;
A laborer but in heart, while bound my hands
Hang idly down still waiting Thy commands.

# 3

## *The Disciple*

Thou wilt my hands employ, though others find
No work for those who praise Thy name aright;
And in their worldly wisdom call them blind,
Whom Thou hast blest with Thine own Spirit's sight.
But while they find no work for Thee to do,
And blindly on themselves alone rely;
The child must suffer what Thou sufferest too,
And learn from him Thou sent e'en so to die;
Thou art my Father, Thou wilt give me aid
To bear the wrong the spirit suffers here;
Thou hast Thy help upon the mighty laid,
In Thee I trust, nor know to want or fear;—
But ever onward walk, secure from sin,
For Thou hast conquered every foe within.

# 4

## *The Clay*

Thou shalt do what Thou wilt with Thine own hand,
Thou forms't the spirit like the moulded clay;
For those who love Thee keep Thy just command,
And in Thine image grow as they obey;
New tints and forms with every hour they take,
Whose life is fashioned by Thy Spirit's power;
The crimson dawn is round them when they wake,
And golden triumphs wait the evening hour;
The queenly-sceptred night their souls receives,
And spreads their pillow 'neath her sable tent;
And o'er their slumbers unseen angels breathe,
Above them Sleep their palm with poppy weaves,
The rest Thou hast to all who labor lent;
That they may rise refreshed to light again,
And with Thee gather in the whitening grain.

# 5

## *He Was Acquainted with Grief*

I cannot tell the sorrows that I feel
By the night's darkness, by the prison's gloom;
There is no sight that can the death reveal
The spirit suffers in a living tomb;
There is no sound of grief that mourners raise,
No moaning of the wind, or dirge-like sea,
Nor hymns, though prophet tones inspire the lays,
That can the spirit's grief awake in thee.
Thou too must suffer as it suffers here
The death in Christ to know the Father's love;
Then in the strains that angels love to hear
Thou too shalt hear the Spirit's song above,
And learn in grief what these can never tell,
A note too deep for earthly voice to swell.

# 6

## *I Was Sick and in Prison*

Thou hast not left the rough-barked tree to grow
Without a mate upon the river's bank;
Nor dost Thou on one flower the rain bestow,
But many a cup the glittering drops has drank;
The bird must sing to one who sings again,
Else would her note less welcome be to hear;
Nor hast Thou bid Thy word descend in vain,
But soon some answering voice shall reach my ear;
Then shall the brotherhood of peace begin,
And the new song be raised that never dies,
That shall the soul from death and darkness win,
And burst the prison where the captive lies;
And one by one new-born shall join the strain,
Till earth restores her sons to heaven again.

# 7

## *Night*

I thank Thee, Father, that the night is near
When I this conscious being may resign;
Whose only task Thy words of love to hear,
And in Thy acts to find each act of mine;
A task too great to give a child like me,
The myriad-handed labors of the day,
Too many for my closing eyes to see,
Thy words too frequent for my tongue to say;
Yet when Thou see'st me burthened by Thy love,
Each other gift more lovely then appears,
For dark-robed night comes hovering from above,
And all Thine other gifts to me endears;
And while within her darkened couch I sleep,
Thine eyes untired above will constant vigils keep.

# 8

## *Life*

It is not life upon Thy gifts to live,
But still with deeper roots grow fixed in Thee;
And when the sun and shower their bounties give
To send out thick-leaved limbs; a fruitful tree,
Whose green head meets the eye for many a mile,
Whose moss-grown trunks their rigid branches rear,
And full-faced fruits their blushing welcome smile
As to its goodly shade our feet draw near;
Who tastes its gifts shall never hunger more,
For 'tis the Father spreads the pure repast,
Who while we eat renews the ready store,
Which at His bounteous board must ever last;
For none the bridegroom's supper shall attend,
Who will not hear and make His word their friend.

# 9

## *The Son*

Father I wait Thy word. The sun doth stand
Beneath the mingling line of night and day,
A listening servant, waiting Thy command
To roll rejoicing on its silent way;
The tongue of time abides the appointed hour,
Till on our ear its solemn warnings fall;
The heavy cloud withholds the pelting shower,
Then every drop speeds onward at Thy call;
The bird reposes on the yielding bough,
With breast unswollen by the tide of song,
So does my spirit wait Thy presence now
To pour Thy praise in quickening life along,
Chiding with voice divine man's lengthened sleep,
    While round the Unuttered Word and Love their
      vigils keep.

# *The Spirit Land*

Father! Thy wonders do not singly stand,
Nor far removed where feet have seldom strayed;
Around us ever lies the enchanted land
In marvels rich to Thine own sons displayed;
In finding Thee are all things round us found;
In losing Thee are all things lost beside;
Ears have we but in vain strange voices sound,
And to our eyes the vision is denied;
We wander in the country far remote,
Mid tombs and ruined piles in death to dwell;
Or on the records of past greatness dote,
And for a buried soul the living sell;
While on our path bewildered falls the night
That ne'er returns us to the fields of light.

## *Change*

Father! there is no change to live with Thee,
Save that in Christ I grow from day to day,
In each new word I hear, each thing I see
I but rejoicing hasten on the way;
The morning comes with blushes overspread,
And I new-wakened find a morn within;
And in its modest dawn around me shed,
Thou hear'st the prayer and the ascending hymn;
Hour follows hour, the lengthening shades descend;
Yet they could never reach as far as me
Did not Thy love their kind protection lend,
And I a child might sleep awhile on Thee;
Till to the light restored by gentle sleep
With new-found zeal I might Thy precepts keep.

# *In Him We Live*

Father! I bless Thy name that I do live,
And in each motion am made rich with Thee,
That when a glance is all that I can give,
It is a kingdom's wealth if I but see;
This stately body cannot move, save I
Will to its nobleness my little bring;
My voice its measured cadence will not try,
Save I with every note consent to sing;
I cannot raise my hands to hurt or bless,
But I with every action must conspire;
To show me there how little I possess,
And yet that little more than I desire;
May each new act my new allegiance prove,
Till in Thy perfect love I ever live and move.

# 13

## The New Man

The hands must touch and handle many things,
The eyes long waste their glances all in vain;
The feet course still in idle, mazy rings,
E'er man himself, the lost, shall back regain
The hand that ever moves, the eyes that see,
While day holds out his shining lamp on high,
And, strait as flies the honey-seeking bee,
Direct the feet to unseen flowers they spy;
These, when they come, the man revealed from heaven,
Shall labor all the day in quiet rest,
And find at eve the covert duly given,
Where with the bird they find sweet sleep and rest,
They shall their wasted strength to health restore,
And bid them seek the morn the hills and fields once
    more.

## *The New Birth*

'Tis a new life;—thoughts move not as they did
With slow uncertain steps across my mind,
In thronging haste fast pressing on they bid
The portals open to the viewless wind
That comes not save when in the dust is laid
The crown of pride that gilds each mortal brow,
And from before man's vision melting fade
The heavens and earth;—their walls are falling now.—
Fast crowding on, each thought asks utterance strong;
Storm-lifted waves swift rushing to the shore,
On from the sea they send their shouts along,
Back through the cave-worn rocks their thunders roar;
And I a child of God by Christ made free
Start from death's slumbers to Eternity.

## *The Father*

Thou who first called me from the sleep of death,
Thee may I ever as my Father love;
In Thee my being find, in Thee my breath,
And never from Thyself again remove;
On Thee alone I wait, and Thee I serve;
Thou art my morn, and noon, and evening hour;
May I from Thy commandments never swerve,
So wilt Thou be to me a heavenly dower;
Friends, brothers, wife, shall all be found in Thee,
Children, whose love for me shall ne'er grow cold;
And Thou the Father still o'er all shall be,
In Thine embrace Thy children ever hold;
In Christ awoke from death's forgotten sleep
Thy hands from harm Thy sons shall ever keep.

## *The Living God*

There is no death with Thee! each plant and tree
In living haste their stems push onward still,
The pointed blade, each rooted trunk we see
In various movement all attest Thy will;
The vine must die when its long race is run,
The tree must fall when it no more can rise;
The worm has at its root his task begun,
And hour by hour his steady labor plies;
Nor man can pause but in Thy will must grow,
And, as his roots within more deep extend,
He shall o'er sons of sons his branches throw,
And to the latest born his shadows lend;
Nor know in Thee disease nor length of days,
But lift his head forever in Thy praise.

# 17

## *Labor and Rest*

Thou need'st not rest: the shining spheres are Thine
That roll perpetual on their silent way,
And Thou dost breathe in me a voice divine,
That tells more sure of Thine eternal sway;
Thine the first starting of the early leaf,
The gathering green, the changing autumn hue;
To Thee the world's long years are but as brief
As the fresh tints that Spring will soon renew.
Thou needest not man's little life of years,
Save that he gather wisdom from them all;
That in Thy fear he lose all other fears,
And in Thy calling heed no other call.
Then shall he be Thy child to know Thy care,
And in Thy glorious Self the eternal Sabbath share.

# 18

## *The Journey*

To tell my journeys, where I daily walk,
These words thou hear'st me use were given me;
Give heed, then, when with thee my soul would talk,
That thou the path of peace it goes may see.
I know nowhere to turn, each step is new,
No wish before me flies to point the way;
But on I travel, with no end in view,
Save that from Him who leads I may not stray.
He knows it all; the turning of the road,
Where this way leads and that, He knows it well,
And finds for me at night a safe abode,
Though I all houseless know not where to dwell.—
And can'st thou tell then where my journeying lies?
If so, thou tread'st with me the same blue skies.

# 19

## *The Garden*

I saw the spot where our first parents dwelt;
And yet it wore to me no face of change,
For while amid its fields and groves, I felt
As if I had not sinned, nor thought it strange;
My eye seemed but a part of every sight,
My ear heard music in each sound that rose,
Each sense forever found a new delight,
Such as the spirit's vision only knows;
Each act some new and ever-varying joy
Did by my Father's love for me prepare;
To dress the spot my ever fresh employ,
And in the glorious whole with Him to share;
No more without the flaming gate to stray,
No more for sin's dark stain the debt of death to pay.

# *The Presence*

I sit within my room and joy to find
That Thou who always loves art with me here,
That I am never left by Thee behind,
But by Thyself Thou keep'st me ever near;
The fire turns brighter when with Thee I look,
And seems a kinder servant sent to me;
With gladder heart I read Thy holy book,
Because Thou art the eyes by which I see;
This aged chair, that table, watch, and door
Around in ready service ever wait;
Nor can I ask of Thee a menial more
To fill the measure of my large estate,
For Thou Thyself, with all a Father's care,
Where'er I turn, art ever with me there.

# II

## FOR THE DISOBEDIENT

## *Enoch*

I looked to find a man who walked with God,
Like the translated patriarch of old;—
Though gladdened millions on His footstool trod,
Yet none with Him did such sweet converse hold;
I heard the wind in low complaint go by
That none its melodies like him could hear;
Day unto day spoke wisdom from on high,
Yet none like David turned a willing ear;
God walked alone unhonored through the earth;
For Him no heart-built temple open stood,
The soul forgetful of her nobler birth
Had hewn Him lofty shrines of stone and wood,
And left unfinished and in ruins still
The only temple He delights to fill.

## *The Jew*

Thou art more deadly than the Jew of old,
Thou hast his weapons hidden in thy speech;
And though thy hand from me thou dost withhold,
They pierce where sword and spear could never reach;
Thou hast me fenced about with thorny talk,
To pierce my soul with anguish while I hear;
And while amid thy populous streets I walk,
I feel at every step the entering spear;
Go, cleanse thy lying mouth of all its guile,
That from the will within thee ever flows;
Go, cleanse the temple thou dost now defile,
Then shall I cease to feel thy heavy blows;
And come and tread with me the path of peace,
And from thy brother's harm forever cease.

## 23

## *The Dead*

I see them, crowd on crowd they walk the earth
Dry, leafless trees no autumn wind laid bare;
And in their nakedness find cause for mirth,
And all unclad would winter's rudeness dare;
No sap doth through their clattering branches flow,
Whence springing leaves and blossoms bright appear;
Their hearts the living God have ceased to know,
Who gives the springtime to th'expectant year;
They mimic life, as if from him to steal
His glow of health to paint the livid cheek;
They borrow words for thoughts they cannot feel,
That with a seeming heart their tongue may speak;
And in their show of life more dead they live
Than those that to the earth with many tears they give.

# 24

## *The Eagles*

The eagles gather on the place of death
So thick the ground is spotted with their wings,
The air is tainted with the noisome breath
The wind from off the field of slaughter brings;
Alas! no mourners weep them for the slain,
But all unburied lies the naked soul;
The whitening bones of thousands strew the plain,
Yet none can now the pestilence control;
The eagles gathering on the carcass feed,
In every heart behold their half-formed prey;
The battened wills beneath their talons bleed,
Their iron beaks without remorse must slay;
Till by the sun no more the place is seen,
Where they who worshipped idol gods have been.

## 25

## *Thy Brother's Blood*

I have no brother,—they who meet me now
Offer a hand with their own wills defiled,
And, while they wear a smooth unwrinkled brow,
Know not that Truth can never be beguiled;
Go wash the hand that still betrays thy guilt;—
Before the spirit's gaze what stain can hide?
Abel's red blood upon the earth is spilt,
And by thy tongue it cannot be denied;
I hear not with the ear,—the heart doth tell
Its secret deeds to me untold before;
Go, all its hidden plunder quickly sell,
Then shalt thou cleanse thee from thy brother's gore,
Then will I take thy gift;—that bloody stain
Shall not be seen upon thy hand again.

## 26

### *Ye Gave Me No Meat*

My brother, I am hungry,—give me food
Such as my Father gives me at his board;
He has for many years been to thee good,
Thou canst a morsel then to me afford;
I do not ask of thee a grain of that
Thou offerest when I call on thee for bread;
This is not of the wine nor olive fat,
But those who eat of this like thee are dead;
I ask the love the Father has for thee,
That thou should'st give it back to me again;
This shall my soul from pangs of hunger free,
And on my parched spirit fall like rain;
Then thou wilt prove a brother to my need,
For in the cross of Christ thou too canst bleed.

# The Still-Born

I saw one born, yet he was of the dead;
    Long since the spirit ceased to give us birth;
For lust to sin, and sin to death had led,
    And now its children people o'er the earth.

And yet he thought he lived, and as he grew
    Looked round upon the world and called it fair;
For of the heaven he lost he never knew,
    Though oft he pined in spirit to be there.

And he lived on, the earth became his home,
    Nor learnt he ought of those who came before;
For they had ceased to wish from thence to roam,
    And for the better land could not deplore.

Time passed, and he was buried; lo! the dust
    From which he first was taken him received;
Yet in his dying hour ne'er ceased his trust,
    And still his soul for something heavenly grieved.

And we will hope that there is One who gave
    The rest he sighed for, but the world denied;
That yet his voice is heard beyond the grave,
    That he yet lives who to our vision died.

## 28

### *The Strangers*

Each careworn face is but a book
    To tell of houses bought or sold;
Or filled with words that mankind took
    From those who lived and spoke of old.

I see none whom I know, for they
    See other things than him they meet;
And though they stop me by the way,
    'Tis still some other one to greet.

There are no words that reach my ear
    Those speak who tell of other things
Than what they mean for me to hear,
    For in their speech the counter rings.

I would be where each word is true,
    Each eye sees what it looks upon;
For here my eye has seen but few,
    Who in each act that act have done.

## *The Poor*

I walk the streets and though not meanly drest,
Yet none so poor as can with me compare;
For none though weary call me in to rest,
And though I hunger none their substance share;
I ask not for my stay the broken reed,
That fails when most I want a friendly arm;
I cannot on the loaves and fishes feed,
That want the blessing that they may not harm;
I only ask the living word to hear,
From tongues that now but speak to utter death;
I thirst for one cool cup of water clear,
But drink the riled stream of lying breath;
And wander on though in my Father's land,
Yet hear no welcome voice, and see no beckoning hand.

## *The Guest*

I knock, but knock in vain; there is no call
Comes from within to bid me enter there;
The selfish owner sits within his hall,
And will not open, will not hear my prayer;
Blessed is the man that doth my call attend,
And rise with anxious haste to see his guest;
For I to all that hear me am a friend,
And where I enter in that house is blest;
O hasten then each mansion to prepare
For Him who blesses all who hear His word,
He shall with them his Father's mansion share;
Eye hath not seen, nor mortal ear hath heard
That which the heart that loves the Lord shall see,
When they within the veil with Him shall be.

## 31

## *The Harvest*

They love me not, who at my table eat;
They live not on the bread that Thou hast given;
The word Thou giv'st is not their daily meat,
The bread of life that cometh down from heaven;
They drink but from their lips the waters dry,
There is no well that gushes up within;
And for the meat that perishes they cry,
When Thou hast vexed their souls because of sin;
Oh send Thy laborers! every hill and field
With the ungathered crop is whitened o'er;
To those who reap it shall rich harvests yield,
In full eared grain all ripened for Thy store;
No danger can they fear who reap with Thee,
Though thick with storms the autumn sky may be.

# *The Fig Tree*

Thou wilt not give me aught though I am poor,
And ask with shivering limbs and hungry cry;
And thinkst that I the winter can endure,
And thou doest not my spirit's wants deny;
But thou art poor; for thou hast nought to give
Of that which is both meat and drink to me;
Thou bidst me on the husks thou feedest live,
And with the rags thou wear'st in comfort be;
The figs my Father bade me on thee seek,
I taste not from thy thorns and brambles high;
He made thee strong, I find thee poor and weak;
He made thee rich, yet thou must of me buy;
Who am but blind, and yet to thee can see;
A servant still, and yet to thee am free.

# 33

## *My Meat and Drink*

I do not need thy food, but thou dost mine;
For this will but the body's want repair,
And soon again for meat like this 'twill pine,
And so be fed by thee with daily care;
But that which I can give thou needs but eat,
And thou shalt find it in thyself to be;
Forever formed within a living meat,
On which to feed will make thy spirit free;
Thou shalt not hunger more, for freely given
The bread on which the spirit daily feeds;
This is the bread that cometh down from heaven,
Of which who eats no other food he needs;
But this doth grow within him day by day,
Increasing more the more he takes away.

## 34

### *The Children*

I saw, strange sight! the children sat at meat,
When they their Parent's face had never known;
Nor rose they when they heard His step, to greet;
But feasted there upon His gifts alone;
'Twas morn, and noon, and evening hour the same;
They heeded not 'twas He who gave them bread;
For they had not yet learned to call His name,
They had been children, but they now were dead;
Yet still their Father, with a father's care,
Early and late stood waiting by their board;
Hoping each hour that they His love could share,
And at His table sit to life restored;
Alas! for many a day and year I stood
And saw them feasting thus yet knew not Him how
    good.

# 35

## *The Prison*

The prison-house is full; there is no cell
But hath its prisoner laden with his chains;
And yet they live as though their life was well,
Nor of its burdening sin the soul complains;
Thou dost not see where thou hast lived so long,—
The place is called the skull where thou dost tread.
Why laugh'st thou, then, why sing the sportive song,
As if thou livest, and know'st not thou art dead.
Yes, thou art dead, the morn breaks o'er thee now,—
Where is thy Father, He who gave thee birth?
Thou art a severed limb, a barren bough,
Thou sleepest in deep caverns of the earth.
Awake! thou hast a glorious race to run;
Put on thy strength, thou hast not yet begun.

## *The Unfaithful Servants*

Thou hast no other hands than those that toil,
In other tasks than what thou giv'st them now;
For these thou hast the others work but spoil,
They idly tear the ground that these would plow;
They have been long employed, and learnt them arts,
The others know and yet were never taught;
False actors saying to themselves their parts,
Till they the gait and living tone have caught;
'Tis but a show these buildings that they rear,
Card-fabrics overblown with every breath;
Their mightiest labor, things that but appear;
An out-seen world, begat to thee by death,
First seen when eye began to cease to see
Nor made before thy hand forgot a hand to be.

# 37

## *The Laborers*

The workmen shall not always work; who builds,
His house shall finish with the last-raised stone;
The last small measure full the vessel fills;
The last step taken and thy journey's done;
But where is he, who but one hour ago,
Lifted with toiling arm the burden nigh?
And he whose vessel to the brim did flow,
Or he who laid his staff and sandals by?
I see them still at work another way,
From those that late thou sawest thus employed;
And heard them each unto the other say,
As to new tasks they bent them overjoyed,
"The sun is rising, haste! that he may see,
When setting every hand from labor free."

# 38

## *The Settler*

When thou art done thy toil, anew art born;
With hands that never touched the spade or plough,
Nor in the furrows strewed the yellow corn,
Or plucked the ripened fruit from off the bough:
Then shall thou work begin;—thy plough and spade
Shall break at early morn the virgin soil;
The swelling hill and thickly wooded glade
With changing aspect own the daily toil;
Thy house shall strike the eye, where none are near,
For thou hast traveled far, where few have trod;
And those who journey hence will taste thy cheer,
And bless thee as a favored one of God;
For He it was Who in this pathless wild,
Upon thy good intent so richly smiled.

# 39

Thou know'st not what thy Lord will say
Thou know'st not Him but He knows thee
And though from here He's far away
Can still thy every action see.

While thou wert busy here and there
So He was here and He is gone
Thou oft hast time enough to spare
But He thy Lord and Master now.

Then quickly do the thing thou wouldst
And quickly say the thing thou't speak
Nor to thyself a moment trust
For he who trusts himself is weak.

## *The Created*

There is naught for thee by thy haste to gain;
'Tis not the swift with Me that win the race;
Through long endurance of delaying pain,
Thine opened eye shall see thy Father's face;
Nor here nor there, where now thy feet would turn,
Thou wilt find Him who ever seeks for thee;
But let obedience quench desires that burn,
And where thou art, thy Father too will be.
Behold! as day by day the spirit grows,
Thou see'st by inward light things hid before;
Till what God is, thyself, His image shows;
And thou dost wear the robe that first thou wore,
When bright with radiance from His forming hand,
He saw thee Lord of all His creatures stand.

## 41

## *The Prodigal*

Where hast thou been my brother? thou art torn,
But scarce the rags conceal thy naked soul;
Thou art from desert still to desert borne,
Nor yet hast learned love's yielding, soft control;
Come, let me o'er thee cast this garment white,
Strip off the filthy rags the world has given;
The son has sent me, that I may invite
The weary to his marriage feast in heaven;
Oh come, for there is all thou want'st prepared,
The flowing bowl that cannot ever dry,
The bread of life with Him who died is shared;
Oh come, thou wilt not my request deny,
And wander on in throny paths to bleed,
And on the husks thou feedest ever feed.

# 42

## *Thy Father's House*

Thou art not yet at home; perhaps thy feet
Are on the threshold of thy father's door,
But still thy journey is not there complete,
If thou canst add to it but one step more;
'Tis not thy house which thou with feet can reach,
'Tis where when wearied they will enter not;
But stop beneath an earthly roof, where each
May for a time find comfort in his lot;
Then called to wander soon again must mourn,
That such frail shelter they should call relief;
And onward seek again that distant bourne,
The home of all the family of grief,
Whose doors by day and night stand open wide
For those who enter there shall evermore abide.

# 43

## *The Absent*

Thou art not yet at home in thine own house,
But to one room I see thee now confined;
Having one hole like rat or skulking mouse,
And as a mole to all the others blind;
Does the great Day find preference when he shines
In at each window lighting every room?
No selfish wish the moon's bright glance confines,
And each in turn the stars faint rays illume;
Within thy sleeping room thou dost abide,
And thou the social parlor does prefer;
Another thou wilt in the cupboard hide,
And this or that's the room for him or her;
But the same sun, and moon with silver face
Look in on all, and lighten every place.

# 44

## *The Narrow Way*

Where this one dwells and that, thou know'st it well,
Each earthly neighbor and each earthly friend;
But He who calls thee has no place to dwell,
And canst thou then thine all unto Him lend?
Canst thou a stranger be, where now well known;
Where now thou oftenest go'st, go nevermore,
But walk the world thenceforth thy way alone,
Broadening the path but little worn before?
Then may'st thou find me, when thou't faint and weak,
And the strait road seems narrower still to grow;
For I will words of comfort to thee speak,
And onward with thee to my home I'll go,
Where thou shalt find a rest in labor sweet,
No friend and yet a friend in all to greet.

# 45

## *To All*

Thou know'st not e'er the way to turn or go,
For He who man would follow turneth not;
Enough for thee that thou thy Lord mayst know,
And canst not for a moment be forgot;
His way is hidden that thine eye may seek,
And in the seeking thou thyself may find;
His voice unheard that thou may'st learn to speak,
His eye unseen to show thee thou art blind;
Then haste thee on, his hidden path explore;
And purge thine ear that thou mayst hear his voice;
Unseal thine eye to him who walks before,
And that thou hast a friend unseen in me rejoice;
And follow on though now thy feet may tread,
Where clouds still hang above the unnumbered dead.

# 46

## *The Way*

To good thou askst the way—enter the street,
This is the broad high-way that many tread;
Go follow him whom first thine eye shall meet,
Here is his store, go in; behold thy bread;
Thou turnst away; well, follow him whose ship
Has just returned deep-laden from afar;
Look, see his face how gladdened at the trip.
Is there aught here the good thou seekst, to mar?
Thou trackest one and all, yet find'st it not;
Then learn that *all* are seekers here below;
And let the lesson never be forgot,
That none the path to happiness can show,
Save He whose way is hidden; only known
To those who seek His love, and His alone.

# 47

## *The Sower*

To want is there to be where I am not,
Abundance waits for me where'er I tread;
The cares of life in me are all forgot,
I have enough and e'en to spare of bread;
Come, taste, and hunger shall be laid at rest;
And thirst once quenched shall never thirst again;
Thou shalt of all I have be long possest,
And long thy life my body shall sustain;
There are who food will give thee, but 'tis theirs;
And hunger rages but the more 'tis fed;
'Twas made from out the grains of scattered tares,
That through my field by wicked hands were spread;
But thou shalt have the wheat that's sown by me,
And in thy bosom's field new harvests ever see.

# 48

## *Jacob's Well*

Thou pray'st not, save when in thy soul thou pray'st;
Disrobing of thyself to clothe the poor;
The words thy lips shall utter then, thou say'st;
They are as marble, and they shall endure;
Pray always; for on prayer the hungry feed;
Its sound is hidden music to the soul,
From low desires the rising strains shall lead,
And willing captives own thy just control;
Draw not too often on the gushing spring,
But rather let its own o'erflowings tell,
Where the cool waters rise, and thither bring
Those who more gladly then will hail the well;
When gushing from within new streams like thine,
Shall bid them ever drink and own its source divine.

# 49

## *The Eye and Ear*

Thou readest, but each lettered word can give
Thee but the sound that thou first gave to it;
Thou lookest at the page, things move and live
In light thine eye and thine alone has lit;
Ears are there yet unstopped, and eyes unclosed,
That see and hear as in one common day;
When they which present see have long reposed,
And he who hears has mouldered too to clay;
These ever see and hear; they are in Him,
Who speaks, and all is light; how dark before!
Each object throws aside its mantle dim,
Which hid the starry robe that once it wore;
And shines full born disclosing all that is,
Itself by all things seen and owned as His.

# 50

## *Yourself*

'Tis to yourself I speak; you cannot know
Him whom I call in speaking such a one,
For you beneath the earth lie buried low,
Which he alone as living walks upon:
You may at times have heard him speak to you,
And often wished perchance that you were he;
And I must ever wish that it were true,
For then you could hold fellowship with me:
But now you hear us talk as strangers, met
Above the room wherein you lie abed;
A word perhaps loud spoken you may get,
Or hear our feet when heavily they tread;
But he who speaks, or him who's spoken to,
Must both remain as strangers still to you.

## 51

### *Thy Neighbor*

I am thy other self, what thou wilt be,
When thou art I, the one thou seest now;
In finding thy true self thou wilt find me,
The springing blade, where now thou dost but plow.
I am thy neighbor, a new house I've built,
Which thou as yet hast never entered in;
I come to call thee; come in when thou wilt,
The feast is always waiting to begin.
Thou shouldst love me, as thou dost love thyself,
For I am but another self beside;
To show thee him thou lov'st in better health,
What thou wouldst be, when thou to him has died;
Then visit me, I make thee many a call;
Nor live I near to thee alone, but all.

# 52

## *The Slaveholder*

When comes the sun to visit thee at morn,
Art thou prepared to give him welcome then;
Or is the day that with his light is born,
With thee a day that has already been;
Hast thou filled up its yet unnumbered hours
With selfish thoughts and made them now thine own?
Then for thee cannot bloom its budding flowers,
The day to thee hast past, and onward flown;
The noon may follow with its quickening heat,
The grain grow yellow in its ripening rays;
And slow-paced evening mark the noon's retreat,
Yet thou as dead to them live all thy days;
For thou hast made of God's free gifts a gain,
And would'st the sovereign day a slave in bonds retain.

# 53

## *The Morning Watch*

'Tis near the morning watch, the dim lamp burns
But scarcely shows how dark the slumbering street;
No sound of life the silent mart returns;
No friends from house to house their neighbors greet;
It is the sleep of death; a deeper sleep
Than e'er before on mortal eyelids fell;
No stars above the gloom their places keep;
No faithful watchmen of the morning tell;
Yet still they slumber on, though rising day
Hath through their windows poured the awakening
  light;
Or, turning in their sluggard trances, say—
"There yet are many hours to fill the night;"
They rise not yet; while on the bridegroom goes
'Till he the day's bright gates forever on them close!

## 54

### *Flee to the Mountains*

The morn is breaking   see the rising sun
Has on your windows cast his burning light
Arise   the day is with you   onward run
Lest soon you wander lost in murky night
I will be with you 'tis your day of flight
Hasten   the hour is near   you cannot fly
Leave all for me   who stops can never fight
The foe that shall assail him from on high
They come   the plagues that none can flee
Behold   the wrath of God is on you poured
O hasten   find the rest He gives in me
And you shall fear no fear in me restored
They cannot pause   O hasten while you may
For soon shall close around thy little day.

# 55

## *The Snare*

My kingdom is within you  haste to find
Its glorious dawn bright streaming in the west
Open thine inward eye for thou art blind
Behold the morning waits  go cleanse thy breast
For see its herald  he who goes before
And with his warning voice prepares the way
Quick o'er your hearts his cleansing water pour
And you shall see the rising of my day
Go not from place to place  it comes not so
But as the lightning shineth from the east
And to the west its forked branches go
E'en so unnoticed has its light increased
Till in its circling brightness all shall stand
And none escape who slight John's true command.

# 56

## *Christmas*

Awake ye dead! the summons has gone forth,
That bids ye leave the dark enclosing grave;
From east to west 'tis heard, from south to north
The word goes forth the imprisoned souls to save;
Though ye have on the garments of the dead,
And the fourth day have slept within the earth,
Come forth! you shall partake the living bread,
And be a witness of the spirit's birth;
Awake ye faithful! throw your grave-clothes by,
He whom you seek is risen, he bids you rise;
The cross again on earth is lifted high,
Turn to its healing sight your closing eyes;
And you shall rise and gird your armor on,
And fight till you a crown in Christ have won.

## 57

### *Who Hath Ears to Hear Let Him Hear*

The sun doth not the hidden place reveal,
Whence pours at morn his golden flood of light;
But what the night's dark breast would fain conceal,
In its true colors walks before our sight;
The bird does not betray the secret springs,
Whence note on note her music sweetly pours;
Yet turns the ear attentive while she sings,
The willing heart while falls the strain adores;
So shall the spirit tell not whence its birth,
But in its light thine untold deeds lay bare;
And while it walks with thee flesh-clothed the earth,
Its words shall of the Father's love declare;
And happy those whose ears shall hail its voice,
And clean within the day it gives rejoice.

# III

## SONG

# 58

## *The Fair Morning*

The clear bright morning, with its scented air
And gaily waving flowers, is here again;
Man's heart is lifted with the voice of prayer,
And peace descends, as falls the gentle rain;
The tuneful birds, that all the night have slept,
Take up, at dawn, the evening's dying lay;
When sleep upon their eyelids gently crept
And stole, with stealthy craft, their song away.
High overhead the forest's swaying boughs
Sprinkle with drops the traveler on his way,
He hears far off the tinkling bells of cows
Driven to pasture at the break of day;
With vigorous step he passes swift along,
Making the woods reecho with his song.

# 59

## *The Clouded Morning*

The morning comes, and thickening clouds prevail,
Hanging like curtains all the horizon round,
Or overhead in heavy stillness sail,
So still is day, it seems like night profound,
Scarce by the city's din the air is stirred,
And dull and deadened comes its every sound;
The cock's shrill, piercing voice subdued is heard,
By the thick folds of muffling vapors drowned.
Dissolved in mists the hills and trees appear,
Their outlines lost and blended with the sky;
And well-known objects, that to all are near,
No longer seem familiar to the eye;
But with fantastic forms they mock the sight,
As when we grope amid the gloom of night.

# 60

## *Morning*

The light will never open sightless eyes,
It comes to those who willingly would see;
And every object, hill, and stream, and skies,
Rejoice within th' encircling line to be;
'Tis day—the field is filled with busy hands,
The shop resounds with noisy workmen's din,
The traveler with his staff already stands
His yet unmeasured journey to begin;
The light breaks gently, too, within the breast—
Yet there no eye awaits the crimson morn,
The forge and noisy anvil are at rest,
Nor men nor oxen tread the fields of corn,
Nor pilgrim lifts his staff—it is no day
To those who find on earth their place to stay.

# 61

## *The Lost*

The fairest day that ever yet has shone,
Will be when thou the day within shalt see;
The fairest rose that ever yet has blown,
When thou the flower thou lookest on shalt be.
But thou art far away among Time's toys;
Thyself the day thou lookest for in them,
Thyself the flower that now thine eye enjoys,
But wilted now thou hang'st upon thy stem.
The bird thou hearest on the budding tree,
Thou hast made sing with thy forgotten voice;
But when it swells again to melody,
The song is thine in which thou wilt rejoice;
And thou new risen 'midst these wonders live,
That now to them dost all thy substance give.

# 62

## *The True Light*

The morning's brightness cannot make thee glad,
If thou art not more bright than it within;
And nought of evening's peace hast thou e'er had,
If evening first did not with thee begin.
Full many a sun I saw first set and rise,
Before my day had found a rising too;
And I with Nature learned to harmonize,
And to her times and seasons made me true.
How fair that new May morning when I rose
Companion of the sun for all the day;
O'er every hill and field where now he goes,
With him to pass, nor fear again to stray;
But 'neath the full-orbed moon's reflected light
Still onward keep my way till latest night.

# 63

## *To the Pure All Things Are Pure*

The flowers I pass have eyes that look at me,
The birds have ears that hear my spirit's voice,
And I am glad the leaping brook to see,
Because it does at my light step rejoice.
Come, brothers, all who tread the grassy hill,
Or wander thoughtless o'er the blooming fields,
Come learn the sweet obedience of the will;
Thence every sight and sound new pleasure yields,
Nature shall seem another house of thine,
When He who formed thee, bids it live and play,
And in thy rambles e'en the creeping vine
Shall keep with thee a jocund holiday,
And every plant, and bird, and insect, be
Thine own companions born for harmony.

# 64

## *The Stranger's Gift*

I found far culled from fragrant field and grove
Each flower that makes our Spring a welcome guest;
In one sweet bond of brotherhood inwove
An osier band their leafy stalks compressed;
A stranger's hand had made their bloom my own,
And fresh their fragrance rested on the air;
His gift was mine—but he who gave unknown,
And my heart sorrowed though the flowers were fair.
Now oft I grieve to meet them on the lawn,
As sweetly scattered round my path they grow,
By One who on their petals paints the dawn,
And gilt with sunset splendors bids them glow,
For I ne'er asked 'who steeps them in perfume?'
Nor anxious sought His love who crowns them all
    with bloom.

# 65

## *The Latter Rain*

The latter rain, it falls in anxious haste
Upon  the sun-dried fields and branches bare,
Loosening with searching drops the rigid waste
As if it would each root's lost strength repair;
But not a blade grows green as in the spring,
No swelling twig puts forth its thickening leaves;
The robbins only mid the harvests sing
Pecking the grain that scatters from the sheaves;
The rain falls still—the fruit all ripened drops,
It pierces chestnut burr and walnut shell,
The furrowed fields disclose the yellow crops,
Each bursting pod of talents used can tell,
And all that once received the early rain
Declare to man it was not sent in vain.

# 66

## *The Cottage*

The house my earthly parent left,
My heavenly Father still throws down;
For 'tis of air and sun bereft,
Nor stars its roof with beauty crown.

He gave it me, yet gave it not;
As one whose gifts are wise and good;
'Twas but a poor and clay-built cot,
And for a time the storms withstood.

But lengthening years and frequent rain
O'ercame its strength, it tottered, fell;
And left me homeless here again.
And where to go I could not tell.

But soon the light and open air,
Received me as a wandering child;
And I soon thought their house more fair,
And all my grief their love beguiled.

Mine was the grove, the pleasant field,
Where dwelt the flowers I daily trod;
And there beside them too I kneeled
And called their friend, my Father, God.

# 67

## *To-Day*

I live but in the Present, where art thou?
Hast thou a home in some past, future year?
I call to thee from every leafy bough,
But thou art far away, and canst not hear.

Each flower lifts up its red, or yellow head,
And nods to thee, as thou art passing by;
Hurry not on, but stay thine anxious tread,
And thou shalt live with me, for here am I.

The brook that murmurs by thee, heed its voice,
Nor stop thine ear, 'tis I that bid it flow;
And thou with its glad waters shalt rejoice,
And of the life I live within them know.

And hill, and grove, and flowers, and running stream,
When thou dost live with them shall look more fair;
And thou awake, as from a cheating dream,
The life to-day with me and mine to share.

# 68

## *Faith and Sight*

The comings on of Faith,
　　The goings out of Sight;
Are as the brightening of the morn,
　　The dying of the night.

Man tells not of the hour,
　　By Him alone 'tis told;
Who day and night with certain bounds,
　　Marked out for him of old.

The singing of the bird,
　　The sinking of her strain;
The roar of ocean's storm-tost wave,
　　And lull, the date retain.

The fading of the leaf,
　　The blending of each hue;
The hour still hold in truth,
　　When change the old and new.

There's nought in Nature's hymn,
　　Of earth, or sea, or sky;
But is prophetic of the time
　　When birth to death is nigh.

# 69

## *The Dwellings of the Just*

I saw the dwellings of the Just,
　　No sun was in their sky;
Nor candle lit their rooms by night,
　　They saw without an eye.

They walked upright as fearing none,
　　Each step so true they trod;
They moved as those who have been taught
　　The perfect-law of God.

All day they labored, yet at rest,
　　As in His sight who lives;
Who to each one his rightful place,
　　And rightful portion gives.

And shadowy night was blessed to them,
　　As His who gives the day;
And sweet the sleep it brought to these,
　　Whose joy was to obey.

# 70

## *The Call*

Why art thou not awake, my son?
The morning breaks I formed for thee;
And I thus early by thee stand,
Thy new-awakening life to see.

Why art thou not awake, my son?
The birds upon the bough rejoice;
And I thus early by thee stand,
To hear with theirs thy tuneful voice.

Why sleep'st thou still? the laborers all
Are in my vineyard;—hear them toil,
As for the poor with harvest song,
They treasure up the wine and oil.

I come to wake thee; haste, arise,
Or thou no share with me can find;
Thy sandals seize, gird on thy clothes,
Or I must leave thee here behind.

# 71

## *The Word*

The Word where is it? hath it voice,
That I may hear it and be free;
Hath it a form, that I may know;
A touch, that I may feel; and see?

Where does it dwell? above, below?
Or is it where e'en now I tread?
I would be near it when it calls,
And bids awake the slumbering dead.

'Tis near me; yet I hear it not—
That voice that cometh down from heaven—
And hide myself in shrinking fear,
When wide above the earth is riven.

Oh strengthen in me faith to rise,
And go where'er it leads the way;
That I may live with it as one,
And all that it commands obey.

## 72

### The Coming of the Lord

"Take ye heed, watch and pray: for ye know
not when the time is."

Mark 13:33.

Come suddenly, O Lord, or slowly come,
    I wait Thy will, Thy servant ready is;
Thou hast prepared Thy follower a home,
    The heaven in which Thou dwellest too is his.

Come in the morn, at noon, or midnight deep,
    Come, for Thy servant still doth watch and pray;
E'en when the world around is sunk in sleep,
    I wake, and long to see Thy glorious day.

I would not fix the time, the day, nor hour,
    When Thou with all Thine angels shalt appear;
When in Thy kingdom Thou shalt come with power,
    E'en now, perhaps, the promised day is near!

For though, in slumber deep, the world may lie,
    And e'en Thy Church forget Thy great command;
Still year by year Thy coming draweth nigh,
    And in its power Thy kingdom is at hand.

Not in some future world alone 'twill be,
    Beyond the grave, beyond the bounds of time;
But on the earth Thy glory we shall see,
    And share Thy triumph, peaceful, pure, sublime.

Lord! help me that I faint not, weary grow,
    Nor at Thy Coming slumber too, and sleep;
For Thou hast promised, and full well I know
    Thou wilt to us Thy word of promise keep.

## 73

### *The Immortal*

'Tis not that Thou hast given me
A form which mortals cannot see,
    That I rejoice;
But that I know Thou art around,
And though there comes to me no sound,
    I hear Thy voice.

'Tis not that Thou hast given me place
Among a new and happy race,
    I serve Thee, Lord;
But that Thy mercies never fail,
And shall o'er all my songs prevail,
    Through Thine own word.

Its praise has gone abroad; who hears,
He casts aside all earthly fears,
    By it he lives;
It bids him triumph o'er the grave,
And him o'er death dominion gave,—
    Thy joy and peace it gives.

Hear it, ye poor! and ye who weep!
Arise, who lie in sin's long sleep!
    'Tis strong to free;
Give ear and it shall lead you on,
Till you the crown again have won,
    And me and mine can see.

# 74

## *The Fox and the Bird*

The bird that has no nest,
The Fox that has no hole;
He's wiser than the rest,
Her eggs are never stole.

She builds where none can see,
He hides where none can find;
The bird can rest where'er she be,
He freely moves as wind.

Thou hast not found her little young,
E'en though thou'st sought them long;
Though from thine earliest day they've sung,
Thou hast not heard their song.

Thou hast not found that Fox's brood,
That nestle under ground;
Though through all time his burrow's stood,
His whelps thou'st never found.

# 75

## *The Prayer*

Wilt Thou not visit me?
The plant beside me feels Thy gentle dew;
　　And every blade of grass I see,
From Thy deep earth its moisture drew.

Wilt Thou not visit me?
Thy morning calls on me with cheering tone;
　　And every hill and tree
Lend but one voice, the voice of Thee alone.

Come, for I need Thy love,
More than the flower the dew or grass the rain;
　　Come, gently as Thy holy dove;
And let me in Thy sight rejoice to live again.

I will not hide from them,
When Thy storms come, though fierce may be their wrath,
　　But bow with leafy stem,
And strengthened follow on Thy chosen path.

Yes, Thou wilt visit me;
Nor plant nor tree Thy eye delights so well,
　　As when from sin set free,
My spirit loves with Thine in peace to dwell.

# NOTES TO INTRODUCTION

1. The Rev. James Freeman Clarke says in his brief biographical preface to *Poems and Essays* (Boston, 1886), "To Jones Very success or failure was a thing of little consequence, for that was in the hands of the Lord. His only concern was to submit his will altogether to the Divine Will, and be led by God in all things, great and small" (p. xxiv).

2. As cited from Emerson's Journals by W. P. Andrews in *Poems by Jones Very* (Boston, 1883), p. 13.

3. W. P. Andrews offers a luminous portrait of Very in his "Memoir" to *Poems by Jones Very*. William Irving Bartlett has written the one book-length biography of Very, *Jones Very: Emerson's "Brave Saint"* (Durham, 1942). The Essex Institute in Salem has a helpful genealogical article, "The Very Family," *Essex Institute Historical Collections* (Salem, 1859), pp. 33–38.

4. The Very household included the poet's mother, his sisters, Frances and Lydia Louisa, and his brother, Washington. Lydia Louisa was a poet and school teacher; Washington, who died in 1853, graduated with honors from Harvard in 1843, was ordained, and finally taught a private school in Salem. Cf. Bartlett, p. 120.

The Houghton Library at Harvard and the Harris Collection of American Poetry at Brown University contain the unpublished manuscripts of Very's sermons.

5. Very's "commonplace" books are in the Archives of Widener

Library at Cambridge. All subsequent references in text and footnotes are to these books.

6. Cf. the earliest "commonplace" book, begun before Very entered Harvard: "I determined to read over the Latin authors in order; and read this year Virgil, Sallust, Livy, Velleius Paterculus, Valerius Maximus, Tacitus, Suetonius, Quintus Curtius, Justin, Florus, Plautus, Terence, Lucretius."

7. Archives of Widener Library. *Bowdoin Prize Dissertations*, Vol. VI, No. 2.

There are, of course, thematic parallels in Very to Milton's "How Soon Hath Time" and "On His Blindness."

8. "National Literature," *Channing's Works* (Boston, 1886), p. 135. Further references to works by William Ellery Channing are from this volume.

9. *Essays and Poems* (Boston, 1839), p. 79. William James says, with apparent endorsement, "Some say that the capacity or incapacity for it [surrender] is what divides the religious from the merely moralistic character." *Varieties of Religious Experience* (New York, 1902), p. 108. "Surrender" thus becomes a common denominator to all religious experiences. Very is distinguished by a sole insistence upon it.

10. "Shakespeare," p. 79.

11. *Essays and Poems*, p. 28.

12. Ms. letter to Rev. H. W. Bellows, Massachusetts Historical Society. Salem, 29 December 1838. I have reproduced Very's punctuation and underlining.

13. The reference is unquestionably to his apocalyptic cry in class, just before he left Harvard: "Flee to the mountains for the end of all things is at hand!" Cf. the poem, "Flee to the Mountains."

14. Cf. John 3:30. The concept of the "new birth" has central significance for Very. Though it originates in Christ's words to Nicodemus, it was specially emphasized by the mystics, Johannes Tauler and Meister Eckhart; and it suggests a peculiarly Edwardsean or Wesleyan distinction.

15. Ms. Samuel Gray Ward. An account of a visit from Jones Very, probably in 1839. Massachusetts Historical Society.

16. Clarke, p. xxv. Compare Very's attitude with the following comment by the nineteenth-century Hindu saint, Sri Ramakrishna. "A man who has realized God shows certain characteristics. He becomes like a child or a madman or an inert thing or a ghoul. Further, he is firmly convinced that he is the machine and God is its Operator."

17. Emerson's account, as quoted in Andrews's "Memoir," p. 17.

18. Andrews, p. 18. "He finally called on the different members of the profession and offered to pray with them, that they too might submit themselves wholly to the Divine Will and be baptized with the Holy Ghost." Andrews also quotes Emerson's amusing account of a meeting with a local preacher. "The preacher began to tower and dogmatize with many words. Then I foresaw that his doom was fixed; and, as soon as he had ceased speaking, the Saint set him right, and blew away all his words in an instant,—unhorsed him, I may say, and tumbled him along the ground in utter dismay, like my angel of Heliodorus; never was discomfiture more complete" (p. 15).

19. Ronald Knox, *Enthusiasm* (Oxford, 1950), p. 271. "What irritates the reader, as he probes the writings of the Quietists to see where Quietism goes wrong, is not any proposition or set of propositions; it is the *temper* which seems to be continually claiming that they have a monopoly of the love of God." Knox offers a particularly shrewd analysis of Quietism (Chapters XI–XIV). I quarrel with his use of the near-fanatic Mme. Guyon as his chief paradigm, and his overemphasis on the "political" defeat of Fénelon by Bossuet, without studying Fénelon's richness.

20. Very attended Emerson's lectures, Margaret Fuller's "conversations," held at George Ripley's house, and "Hedge's Club" meetings. He thus associated for a time with Bronson Alcott, Stearns Wheeler, James Freeman Clarke, and Cyrus Bartol, among others. But Very has only minor ideological affinities with the Transcendentalists. There are three important essays which compare Very with either Emerson or the Tran-

123

scendentalists: Carlos Baker, "Emerson and Jones Very," *New England Quarterly*, VII (1934), 90–99; Yvor Winters, "Jones Very and R. W. Emerson," *Maule's Curse* (Norfolk, 1938), pp. 125–46; Warner B. Berthoff, "Jones Very: New England Mystic," *Boston Public Library Quarterly*, II (1950), 63–76.

21. Cf. Knox, p. 351. ". . . the idea of 'losing yourself in God' is common to Quietist and mystic; 'I am no longer alive, it is Christ that lives in me.' But the Quietist has an emphasis all his own; he proceeds to *identify* himself with Christ. 'The good man,' said Eckhart, 'is the only begotten Son of God.' " Very's identification with Christ is complete in such poems as "Flee to the Mountains" and "The Snare."

22. Ms. Sermon #12. Houghton Library, Harvard. John 1 and Gen. 1. "The Word existing before the Universe."

23. Cf. "The Absent."

24. Ms. Letter to Emerson. Salem, 30 November 1838. Wellesley Library. "The believing which the kingdom requires is *being*."

25. *Journals of Ralph Waldo Emerson*, ed. Edward Waldo Emerson and Waldo Emerson Forbes (Boston, 1911), V, 220–21. "Here is Simeon the Stylite, or John of Patmos, in the shape of Jones Very, religion for religion's sake, religion divorced, detached from man, from the world, from science and art; grim, unmarried, insulated, accusing; yet true in itself, and speaking things in every word. The lie is in the detachment; and when he is in the room with other persons, speech stops as if there were a corpse in the apartment."

26. Cf. Emerson's "Divinity School Address." And note in the following journal entry for 5 November 1845 Emerson's insistence upon the *mythology* of Christianity, as well as his final quarrel with Very: "*Swedenborg*. He reminds me again and again of our Jones Very, who had an illumination that enabled him to excel everybody in wit and to see farthest in every company and quite easily to bring the proudest to confusion; and yet he could never get out of his Hebraistic phraseology and mythology, and, when all was over, still remained in the thin porridge or cold tea of Unitarianism." (*Journals*, VII, 136–37.)

27. Ms. Sermon #1. Houghton Library, Harvard. Luke 24:5. "Do we not need a belief in the Resurrection to give to our Chy power and sanctity. . . . Have we not separated Chy too much from Christ? Is it not faith in Him, as risen from the dead, that gives to his teachings meaning and authority?"

28. Bartlett, p. 43.

29. There are several such mss. in the Harris Collection of American Poetry at Brown University.

30. For example, "nature/Through all her works proclaims it, from the orbs,/That wheel their courses through the void immense,/To insect fluttering in the summer's breeze,/All, all proclaim the destiny of man." "Lines," in Bartlett, p. 186.

31. Ms. Letter to Tuckerman. Salem, 1861. Houghton Library, Harvard. Though Very claimed he was not a literary man, he wrote hundreds of poems, and eventually began to order and number them by groups, possibly for publication. Still, he is justified in his claim. Except for some hymns—which often are strikingly beautiful—Very's later poems are occasional and undistinguished. He wrote sonnets on the potato blight, the camphene lamp, the Nebraska Bill, State's rights, the East India Marine Museum, a series on the Puritans, and several dozen dull tributes to dead friends.

32. *Principles of the Interior or Hidden Life*, an immensely interesting devotional book, should be closely read by anyone who studies Very's sermons. Austin Warren, in "Fénelon among the Anglo-Saxons," *New England Saints* (Ann Arbor, 1956), pp. 68–69, comments on the wide influence of Upham's works.

33. Ms. Sermon #9. Houghton Library, Harvard. John 1:18.

34. Ms. Sermon #23. Houghton Library, Harvard. John 20:24–29.

35. Ms. Sermon #37. Houghton Library, Harvard. Parable of the Sower.

36. Ms. Sermon #31. Houghton Library, Harvard. Matt. 5:13. And Ms. Sermon #29. John 15:5.

37. Ms. Sermon #33. Houghton Library, Harvard. Acts 12:11.

"The Christian's trust in the Lord does not beget a vain confidence or foolish expectation; but patience, submission, and humble dependence upon Him who orders all his lot for his best good. He will see God's angel where others, who slumber and sleep like guards of the prison, see nothing; or only what appears to them a natural event." "The Scriptures were not given to make us credulous or superstitious; but to save us from presumption, and the dominion of the senses."

38. Ms. Sermon #39. Houghton Library, Harvard. I Cor. 6:30. "Glorify God in your body."

39. Ms. Sermon #43. Houghton Library, Harvard. John 14:22-24.

40. Ms. Sermon #3. Harris Collection, Brown University. John 1:4. And, Ms. Sermon #1. Houghton Library, Harvard. Luke 24:5. "A merely intellectual belief, or assent, based on what is demonstrated or proved, is not the highest faith. It may have no quickening, vivifying power." "We need that prayer of the heart . . ."

41. Ms. Sermon #31. Houghton Library, Harvard. Matt. 5:13. "Ye are the Salt of the Earth. But if the Salt have lost its savor, wherewith shall it be salted?"

42. P. 294.

43. Ms. "An Epistle on Miracles." Sent to Emerson in 1842. Wellesley Library. "Instead of understanding that this person who speaks to you is external to the you he addressed from *within*, you transfer this power to an external influence over your visible bodies as you call them and believe that these are to be raised by him after their decay . . ."

44. Clarke, "Progress," p. 221.

45. "Shakespeare," pp. 56–57. Very speaks of Shakespeare's "power of adapting himself to his characters"; later (p. 75) he says, "No man can enter more entirely into the lives of others than Shakespeare has done until he has laid down his own life and gone forth to seek and save that which is lost." Here Very misleadingly links a religious with an aesthetic process; for him, surrender was a personal act of devotion, as it must be—it may have given him spiritual communion with others, but it did not allow him to depict their earthly image and drama.

Warner B. Berthoff, *op. cit.*, p. 71, admirably suggests, Very "saw nothing in matter, which of itself could partake of spirit, nothing in man which of itself might lead him to God. God was not in man unless He entered him totally, so that man was no longer anything in himself. An infinite qualitative distinction remained: man was either dead in the flesh or alive in the spirit."

46. For example, these lines from "The Barberry Bush": "Upon the hills of Salem scattered wide,/Their yellow blossoms gain the eye of spring," and, from "Nature," "Nature! my love for thee is deeper far/ Than strength of words though spirit born can tell." In "The Wind-flower," the image is used as a tepid lesson: the flower looks up with meek confiding eye, and so should we. Some unsuccessful poems contain startlingly fine lines. But these usually relate to his Quietist paradox, such as the superb, "A motion that scarce knows itself from rest," in the otherwise dull "Nature."

47. Norton's comment is quoted in Andrews, p. 29.

48. Knox, p. 270. Rev. J. P. de Caussade, S.J., presents a similar, and apt caution. "Books, wise counsels, vocal prayers, interior affections, if they come to us in the order of God, instruct, guide, and unite the soul to Him. Quietism errs when it disclaims these means and all sensible appearances, for there are souls whom God wills shall be always led in this way, and their state and their attractions clearly indicate it. In vain we picture to ourselves methods of abandonment whence all action is excluded. When the order of God causes us to act, our sanctification lies in action." *Abandonment*, trans. Ella McMahon, ed. Rev. H. Ramière, S.J. (New York, 1887), pp. 55–56.

49. Since virtually all of the better poems are sonnets, division by form is inappropriate; chronological sequence must be discounted because precise dating is impossible, and most of Very's poems used here were written in a short period. W. P. Andrews, despite his prudent selection, begs the issue by establishing six categories "With a view of showing the development of the Author's religious idea connectedly": "The Call," "The New Birth," "The Message," "Nature," "Song and

Praise," and "The Beginning and the End." Clarke follows distinctions begun by Very on sheets left among his manuscript poems: "Poems," "Religious Sonnets," "The Puritans," "Hymns," "Poems Descriptive of Nature," "Political Sonnets," "Miscellaneous Poems." But there is no distinction between "Poems" and "Religious Sonnets" apparent in Clarke's edition, and other categories have few if any worthy poems. I group the poems by stance, the position from which the poet approaches his themes: for his own spiritual life, for that of others, or in song and hymn. There are problems here since, for example, Very's admonition implies both surrender and song, but any grouping of an author's verse must admit a degree of arbitrariness, and this seems the clearest distinction.

# NOTES TO THE POEMS

When available, I have used the last manuscript version of a poem, changing only obvious spelling errors ("riggid" and "chesnut," for example), and regularizing the use of capitals for the pronominal adjective and pronouns referring to the Deity. When there was no manuscript copy of a poem, I generally chose that in the edition of 1839; I preferred Andrews's version to that in Clarke's edition. Emerson was amused and irritated at the arbitrary punctuation in Very; but Very disliked editorializing, even if it improved his poem aesthetically, and at whatever cost I have respected this.

Clarke and Emerson are most loyal to the original, though each adds minor punctuation occasionally, and sometimes standardizes capitalization. But the general carelessness of Clarke's edition makes his text unreliable; haphazard punctuation of the final couplet from "The Unfaithful Servants" obscures the entire poem, and "Faith and Sight" is presented as "Faith and Light." Andrews takes more liberty with the manuscript: his punctuation tightens the original; he uses periods where Very has semicolons, semicolons where Very uses commas.

I have been able to assign outward limits and probable dates, no more, to most of the poems. Between 1836 and 1841 Very published steadily in the *Salem Observer* and the *Western Messenger*. Many of his sonnets were written first in pencil, without punctuation; his later, dated poems, are all punctuated and usually in ink. There are a few obvious instances of revision, but most of the confusion about a final text issues from Very's own neglect of regularized punctuation when making copies of his poems. The original drafts of many early poems appear on the large folded sheets, including as many as thirty-two poems; others are in small booklets. Certain poems in these groups were published early, and it is likely that the others were written within the same period. Very placed the initial "I" below the last line of many early poems sent to the *Salem Observer*; some poems have this mark in manuscript. In several cases, the poems appeared on paper similar to that used for poems sent to the *Western Messenger* and were arranged similarly—four or five poems to a page.

I include dating and publication information for each poem in the following notes. SO is the *Salem Observer* and WM the *Western Messenger*; H Ms refers to the manuscripts in the Houghton Library, and B Ms refers to those in the Harris Collection at Brown; 1839, 1883, 1886, refer to the three editions; the Ms. Ltr. to RWE is in the Wellesley College Library collection. I italicize the version used. The notes are listed by the number of the poem.

1. *1883*, 1886. Compare with Angelus Silesius's lines,

> God is not here or there,
> whoever would him find
> Must seek bound hand and foot,
> bound body, soul, and mind.

—From *The Cherubinic Wanderer*,
trans. Willard Trask.

2. *1883*, 1886. Called "Waiting the Divine Will" in *1886*.

3. WM, Apr. 39; 1839, *1883*, 1886. Cf. Ms. Sermon #23. Houghton Library, Harvard. John 20:27, 28, 29. "They seek not to know by doing the will of God, but of themselves, by their own powers would gain a knowledge of what is hidden from sense."

In *1839*, "Thee" in line 12 is "him," and "Thou" in line 14 is "he." This would transfer the original thanks to the Father, to the Savior.

4. *H Ms*; SO, 20 Apr. 39; 1839, 1883, 1886.

5. WM, Mar. 39; *1839*, 1883, 1886.

6. SO, 29 Jan. 39; *1839*, 1883, 1886.

7. SO, 24 Nov. 38; *1839*, 1883, 1886.

8. *H Ms*; SO, 12 Jan. 39; 1839, 1883, 1886.

9. SO, 17 Nov. 38; *1839*, 1883, 1886.

10. SO, 15 Dec. 38; *1839*, 1883, 1886.

11. *H Ms*; SO, 30 Mar. 39; 1839, 1883, 1886.

12. SO, 10 Nov. 38; *1839*, 1883, 1886. Cf. John 5:30. "I can of mine own self do nothing: as I hear, I judge; and my judgment is just; because I seek not mine own will, but the will of the Father which hath sent me."

13. *1886*. Cf. Eph. 4:24. "And that ye put on the new man, which after God is created in righteousness and true holiness."

14. SO, 27 Oct. 38; *1839*, 1883, 1886.

15. SO, 9 Feb. 39; *1886*. Cf. Ms. Sermon #18. Houghton Library, Harvard. Matt. 6:9. "In calling upon God, as our Father, we feel no longer alone; we enter not only into communion with Him, but with all our fellow beings upon the earth."

16. SO, 22 Dec. 38; *1839*, 1883, 1886. In *1883*, line 1 reads, "There is no death in Thee!"

17. WM, Apr. 39; *1883*.

18. *1883*, 1886.

19. *H Ms*; 1839, 1883, 1886.

20. *H Ms*; SO, 5 Jan. 39; 1839, 1883, 1886.

21. SO, 10 Nov. 38; *1839*, 1883, 1886. Cf. Hebrews 11:5. "By faith Enoch was translated that he should not see death."

22. *H Ms*; SO, 2 Mar. 39; 1839, 1883, 1886.

23. *H Ms*; SO, 5 Jan. 39; 1839, 1883, 1886.

24. *H Ms* (1838?). Cf. Matt. 24:28. "For wheresoever the carcass is, there will the eagles be gathered together."

131

25. SO, 2 Feb. 39; *1839*, 1883, 1886. Cf. Ms. Letter to Emerson, 30 November 1838. Wellesley Library. "When shall we learn that the true return is in the same that we give. That love calls for mercy and not sacrifice. You and others can return me this, and not let me remain alone without a brother in the kingdom."

26. WM, Apr. 39; *1839*, 1883, 1886.

27. *1886*.

28. *1886*.

29. H Ms; SO, 30 Mar. 39; 1839, 1883, 1886.

30. H Ms; 1886.

31. H Ms; SO, 23 Feb. 39; 1883, 1886.

32. H Ms; 1886. Cf. Luke 13:6–9. The poem is an interesting development of the parable of the fig tree. Very actually personifies the tree, addressing it both as tree and person.

33. *WM, Apr. 39.*

34. H Ms (1838?); 1886. The manuscript is signed "I"; the poem was probably written early.

35. WM, Apr. 39; *1883*.

36. H Ms; SO, 18 Jan. 40; 1886.

37. SO, 18 Jan. 40; *1886*. Note how Very's success here depends upon what he does not state; "I see them still at work another way," avoids the direct statement or overstatement that often mars Very's poetry.

38. *WM, Jan. 41.*

39. B Ms (1838?).

40. H Ms (1838?); 1883, 1836. The manuscript is on an "early" sheet.

41. H Ms; 1886.

42. H Ms; 1886.

43. H Ms (1838?); WM, Apr. 41; 1886.

44. *1883*, 1886.

45. H Ms (1838?); 1886.

46. B Ms; 1886.

47. *H Ms* (1838?); 1886. Cf. the Parable of the Sower, Matt. 13:18.

48. *B Ms* (1838?); 1883, 1886. Signed "I." Cf. John 4:6–26. Jesus says: "But whosoever drinketh of the water that I shall give him shall never thirst; but the water that I shall give him shall be in him a well of water springing up into everlasting life."

49. *B Ms*; 1883, 1886.

50. SO, 23 Nov. 39; *1883*, 1886.

51. *H Ms*; SO, 23 Nov. 39; 1886. Also called "Thy Better Self" in manuscript and in *1886*.

52. *B Ms*; 1883, 1886. In the Houghton Library Ms. the poem is called "The Day not for Gain." In 1886, "selfish thoughts" in line 6 is "Thy heart's thoughts."

53. SO, 1 Dec. 38; *1839*, 1883, 1886.

54. *B Ms* (1838?). Cf. Luke 21:21, 22. "Then let them which are in Judea flee to the mountains; and let them which are in the midst of it depart out; and let not them that are in the countries enter thereinto.

"For these be the days of vengeance, that all things which are written may be fulfilled."

55. *B Ms* (1838?).

56. *H Ms*; SO, 10 Feb. 39; 1883, 1886.

57. SO, 6 Apr. 39; *1839*, 1883, 1886.

58. *H Ms*; SO, 21 Sept. 39; 1883, 1886. Line 11 in the manuscript reads, "the bells of tinkling cows"; but I have preferred the line in *1886*.

This poem clearly demonstrates that Very did revise. There are two distinct versions. In *1883* the last six lines read,

> High overhead the forest's swaying boughs
> Sprinkle with drops of dew the whistling boy,
> As to the field he early drives his cows,
> More than content with this his low employ.
> And shall not joy uplift me when I lead
> The flocks of Christ by the still streams to feed?

133

59. *H Ms*; SO, 21 Sept. 39; 1883, 1886.

60. *H Ms*; SO, 23 Mar. 39; 1839, 1883, 1886.

61. SO, 5 Jan. 39; *1883*, 1886.

62. *1883*, 1886.

63. *B Ms* (1838?); *1839*, 1883. The Brown manuscript is unpunctuated. Cf. Titus 1:15.

Compare line 9 with "Man is one world, and hath/Another to attend him" from Herbert's "Man," quoted by Emerson in "Nature."

64. SO, 18 Aug. 38; *1839*, 1883, 1886.

65. *H Ms*; SO, 22 Dec. 38; 1839, 1883, 1886.

66. *Ms Ltr to RWE*; 1839, 1883, 1886. Cf. Very's long, unpublished essay, "The Soul." "We are the immortal guests of the body, a cottage of clay, perishable, belonging to the earth, and which when left by us, crumbles away and decays."

67. *H Ms*; 24 Aug. 39; 1883, 1886.

68. *H Ms*; WH, Apr. 41; 1883, 1886. Incorrectly called "Faith and Light" in *1886*.

69. *H Ms*; WM, Feb. 41.

70. SO, 13 Jul. 39; *1839*, 1883, 1886.

71. *WM, Apr. 41*.

72. *H Ms*; 1883, 1886.

73. SO, 5 Oct. 39; *1883*, 1886.

74. *WM, Apr. 41*. Cf. Luke 9:58. "And Jesus said unto him, Foxes have holes, and birds of the air *have* nests; but the Son of man hath not where to lay *his* head."

75. (1837?); SO, 20 Jul. 39; *1839*, 1883, 1886. In manuscript booklet dated 1837, Harris Collection, without punctuation. Cf. Ms. Sermon #17. Houghton Library, Harvard. James 1:3, 4. "A prayerful dependence upon God makes us to feel that we are laborers with Him; to wait his time, and to trust in His promise."

# A SELECTED BIBLIOGRAPHY

## PRIMARY SOURCES

### Editions

*Essays and Poems.* Boston: Charles C. Little and James Brown, 1839. Sixty-five poems selected and partially edited by Emerson. Contains Very's three essays, "Epic Poetry," "Shakespeare," and "Hamlet." Selected and arranged by Ralph Waldo Emerson, though Emerson's name does not appear as editor.

*Poems and Essays.* Edited by James Freeman Clarke. Boston: Houghton, Mifflin & Co., 1886. Clarke supplies a short but luminous biographical sketch. This is a careless edition which purports to be, but is not, "complete"; among its more than 650 poems are an inordinate number of inferior productions. Twenty-three poems, as Bartlett notes, are repeated.

*Poems by Jones Very.* Edited by W. P. Andrews. Boston: Houghton, Mifflin & Co., 1883. A prudent selection of 138 poems, neatly arranged, with an extremely valuable and sensitive introductory "Memoir."

### Main Manuscript Depositories

Archives, Widener Library, Harvard University. Very's "commonplace" books; his Bowdoin Prize essays; "Individuality," an essay delivered as the English oration at Very's graduation.

Essex Institute, Salem. One sermon; early draught of "Epic Poetry"; miscellaneous papers by and about Very.

Harris Collection of American Poetry, John Hay Library, Brown University. Twenty-eight sermons; poems—unbound, or in booklets; long essay, "The Soul"; miscellaneous papers.

Houghton Library, Harvard. Several hundred poems (transferred from the Andover-Harvard Theological Seminary); several letters by Very.

Houghton Library, Harvard. One hundred and five sermons, bound (transferred from Andover-Harvard Theological Seminary).

Massachusetts Historical Society, Boston. Very's letter to Bellows; Samuel Gray Ward's account of a visit from Very.

Wellesley College Library. Very's formal "Epistles to the Unborn"— sent to Emerson. Letters to Emerson.


## SECONDARY SOURCES

Baker, Carlos. "Emerson and Jones Very," *New England Quarterly*, VII (March, 1934), 90–99. Baker compares Very and Emerson, and attempts to demonstrate and justify Emerson's rejection of the poet.

Bartlett, William Irving. *Jones Very: Emerson's "Brave Saint."* Durham: Duke University Press, 1942. The one biographical study of Very. Most helpful for its many facts on Very's life and ample bibliographical references. Bartlett accurately includes all Very's previously unpublished poems, some of them among his best work.

Berthoff, Warner B. "Jones Very: New England Mystic," *Boston Public Library Quarterly*, II (January, 1950), 63–76. An excellent short essay, concerned chiefly with Very's religious views as revealed in the prose works. Berthoff presents a helpful distillation of Very's themes and makes pertinent contrasts with the Transcendentalists.

Channing, William Ellery. *Works*. Boston: American Unitarian Association, 1886. Channing's theology provides helpful contrasts with

Very's. The most important essays here are: "Self-Culture," "Remarks on National Literature," "Spiritual Freedom," "Likeness to God," "The Imitableness of Christ's Character," "Unitarian Christianity," "The Church," and "Remarks on the Life and Character of Fénelon."

Emerson, Ralph Waldo. *Journals of Ralph Waldo Emerson.* Edited by Edward Waldo Emerson and Waldo Emerson Forbes. 10 vols. Boston: Houghton, Mifflin & Co., 1908–1914. The most penetrating and extended image of Very has been gleaned from Emerson's complete accounts of his relationship with the poet. Bartlett, p. 221, provides a complete list of references to Very in the Journals.

*Fénelon's Letters to Men and Women.* Translated by H. L. Sidney Lear, edited by Derek Stanford. Westminster, Maryland: The Newman Press, 1957. It is extremely interesting to compare Fénelon's patient, firm, and humanistic Quietism with Very's more evangelic brand.

Knox, Ronald A. *Enthusiasm.* Oxford, England: Oxford University Press, 1959. Knox's analysis of Quietism (Chapters XI–XIV) is particularly shrewd and penetrating. His final comments on all religious "enthusiasm" are apt: "In itself enthusiasm is not a wrong tendency but a false emphasis"; "what men like Pascal, Fénelon, and Wesley saw clearly was something true and something valuable"; and "fine instruments are easily spoiled."

Upham, Thomas C. *Principles of the Interior or Hidden Life.* Boston, 1843. Upham, a Professor of Mental and Moral Philosophy at Bowdoin College, drew heavily from Continental Quietism. Very read Upham after his important poems had been written, but there are frequent parallels between the two.

Warren, Austin. *New England Saints.* Ann Arbor: University of Michigan Press, 1956. A hagiography, each chapter of which depicts and studies examples "from four centuries of New England's spiritual life." Most helpful here are "Emerson, Preacher to Himself," and

"Fénelon among the Anglo-Saxons." Very has an historical and spiritual place among Warren's saints.

Winters, Yvor. "Jones Very and R. W. Emerson," *Maule's Curse*. Norfolk: New Directions, 1938. Winters lauds Very as "one of the finest in English," devotional poets and attempts to show his affinity with the Friends and with Edwardsean Calvinism. Much of the essay is devoted to a contrast between Emerson and Very: Emerson, a fraud, relativist, and sentimentalist; Very, a saint and absolutist.

# INDEX TO FIRST LINES AND
# TITLES OF POEMS